Seeds
Of The
Pomegranate

A Sequel To The Pomegranate Pendant

by

Dvora Waysman

Mazo Publishers
Jerusalem, Israel

Seeds Of The Pomegranate

ISBN: 978-965-7344-20-0

Text Copyright © 2007 - Dvora Waysman
Email: ways@netvision.net.il
Website: www.dvorawaysman.com

Published by:
Mazo Publishers
Chaim Mazo, Publisher
P.O. Box 36084
Jerusalem 91360 Israel

Website: www.mazopublishers.com
Email: info@mazopublishers.com

USA Telephone: 1-815-301-3559
Israel Telephone: 054-7294-565

Cover Illustration by Tamar Spero
Cover Layout by Frumi Mazo

Dedication

... With my love and blessings
To 18 wonderful Israeli grandchildren ...

Yosef and Ariel Waysman

Daniel, Jonathan and Assaf Waysman

David, Re'ut, Shir, Amichai and Naomi Lavi

Ta'ir, Shmuel, Shemaya, Hanoch,
Lev, Anya, Miriam and Chana Spero

Acknowledgments

I want to thank all the readers of *The Pomegranate Pendant*, who took it to their hearts. Because so many of you told me that you did not want the story to end, I present this sequel to you.

To my publishers, Chaim and Nechama Mazo, who were with me every step of the way – I truly appreciate your ongoing support.

Special thanks to my grandson, David Lavi, for important suggestions; and to my daughter, Tamar Spero, for the beautiful cover.

About The Author

Dvora Waysman was born Dorothy Opas in Melbourne, Australia. She made *aliyah* with her husband, Zvi, and their four children in 1971 to Israel. She now has 18 Israeli grandchildren.

Today, Dvora makes her home in Jerusalem where she is widely known as a teacher of creative writing. A freelance journalist syndicated worldwide, Dvora is the author of ten books.

In 1981, she was awarded the "For Jerusalem" citation by Mayor Teddy Kollek for her fiction, poetry and features about the city, and in 1988 she received the Seeff Award for Best Foreign Correspondent from the Society for Justice, Ethics and Morals in Journalism.

Dvora has also served as the Press Officer of the Shaare Zedek Medical Center in Jerusalem.

Jerusalem Of Mine

Each day you wait to greet me
Jerusalem of mine –

Your perfume of rosemary and thyme
Wafts down from the hills ...
More seductive than jasmine.
You let me traverse your by-ways
Jerusalem of mine –

Your pine trees filled with birdsong.
Yet sometimes, sighing in the wind,
They remember past sorrows.
Each season has its nuance,
Jerusalem of mine –

Summer a golden girl
Maturing to yellow Autumn.
Winter's white wonderland
Begetting the miracle of Spring.
How do I say "I love you"
Jerusalem of mine?

I have no words, just feelings
That flood my waking moments
With thankfulness and joy.

Part
One

Seeds
Of The
Pomegranate

Chapter 1

WE ARE ALL GATHERED tonight in my family's home in the Jerusalem suburb of Beit Hakerem, the same place I had my henna ceremony in the garden ten years ago.

Tonight, October 20, 1966, is the 10th anniversary of the death of the matriarch of our family, Mazal ben-Yichya. She died on the Hebrew date of Heshvan 15, 5717. We have returned from visiting her grave, but she is not buried where she would have wished, on the Mount of Olives, overlooking her beloved Old City. Sadly, it is occupied by the Jordanians.

Every year, on the anniversary of her death, the *azkera*, or what our Ashkenazi relatives refer to as her *yahrtzeit*, we try to be together, to remember her.

There is not one of us, even the youngest, who does not speak her name in awe. The room is crowded with Mazal's descendants, from her three children – Ruchama, Assaf, and Shalom. They are old now too; but it is our tradition that they re-tell her story every year.

Ruchama always begins, as she is the oldest, already a frail old lady of 83. "Tonight we remember my mother, Mazal ben-Yichya, who left us ten years ago. But she will never really leave us because we all carry part of her in our hearts. She came to Israel as a child-bride of 14 in 1882, the first 'aliyah' (immigration) from Yemen, with our father Ezra. He was a great silversmith and Torah scholar, but died at a young age from typhoid."

As her eyes fill with tears, Assaf takes up the story. "My mother was outstanding," he explains. "She taught herself everything. She learned to speak, read and write several languages, although she had never been to school. After our father died, she supported us all by making the most beautiful jewelry, even though she had never really been apprenticed. She learned from our grandfather Djeddi, of blessed memory, and from our father; and her store 'The Pomegranate Pendant' sustained us all through many years until we had to leave the Old City, and the store was looted and burned to the ground."

Shalom took up the story. "Today we have another family store – "Gargush" – named for the ornate head-dress our Yemenite brides wear on their wedding day. Imma wanted the name 'The Pomegranate Pendant' to die with her after her store was destroyed, unless it could ever be rebuilt in the same place. It was named for the wonderful necklace my father gave her on her wedding night, a golden filigree pomegranate suspended from a thin gold chain. The pomegranate in our tradition symbolizes fruitfulness. She wore it all her life."

I fingered the necklace, which she had placed around my neck at my henna ceremony, a short time before she died. I still remember her words: "Bracha, I am giving you a sacred trust. Every bride in the ben-Yichya family should wear it at her henna ceremony. I know many of them will not marry Yemenites, but perhaps out of respect for my memory, they will maintain the tradition. It is a very lovely one … the dab of henna representing a seal on the hand and heart. Tradition is very important. No one should ever forget where they came from…" She went on to explain about the pendant I still wear today, as beautiful as it was 84 years ago. "The pomegranate, with its many seeds, is a symbol of fruitfulness. I hope, Bracha, that you will be blessed with many children. I would like to think that you will pass it on and that my pomegranate pendant will be a talisman for good, for all the generations yet to come."

I intended to pass it to all the brides in the family, but there had been no more weddings since she died. My own children were only 8, 6 and 4, but among their cousins some were of marriageable age and I would keep the tradition when the time came.

Her prediction that we would not all marry Yemenites had been correct, starting with her own daughter, Ruchama, who had married an Ashkenazi, Menachem Bak-Levi, now deceased. Theirs had been an idyllic marriage, and Ruchama could never speak of him without crying. Many nieces and nephews, and some of her own grandchildren married Ashkenazim and Sephardim. So we sat in my great grandfather Shalom's large dining room in Beit Hakerem, where the yahrtzeit candle burned, and I smiled as I looked around the table. Some of us were olive-skinned, slender and black-haired as our Yemenite heritage suggested. Others were blonde and fair-skinned. We even had a red-head. Such a diverse group, but our common bond was our link to Mazal, who continued to inspire us with her courage and values, a decade after her death. My eight-year-old daughter had been named for her as a second name, and I told and re-told my Shira Mazal about this great lady, for she never tired of stories about her namesake. My two boys, Uri and Moshe, had no patience … their fantasies centered around robots and dinosaurs, but I hoped when they were older, they would listen. My Yemenite husband, Yaacov, whom we called Kobi, had known her briefly and in fact it was he who had suggested naming our first-born Shira Mazal. We hoped she would emulate some of her traits and also that the

name "Mazal" which means "luck" would prove to be pro-
phetic.

We were a noisy family, or maybe it was the number
of people crowded into the room. We had also opened
the doors to the garden, so some of us were on the ve-
randa, but we had all recited the Psalms that spelt out her
name. Now we were eating and drinking, while we caught
up on each other's lives.

My cousins Dina and Yitzhak and their 19-year-old
daughter Dikla had come from the development town of
Rosh haAyin, where there was a large Yemenite community. It is an urban settlement in the Coastal Plain, just a
few minutes east of Petah Tikvah, near the Yarkon River.
In fact, that is how it got its name, for Rosh haAyin means
"Head of the Spring". The springs are still important today in Israel's national water planning. A large British
Army camp built during World War II in 1950 was converted into a shelter for Yemenite immigrants. A year
later, Rosh haAyin was made a permanent settlement.
Most of the inhabitants, including our family, came from
Yemen and today there are 12,000 Yemenites living there
although most of them work in nearby Petah Tikvah in
various industries.

So much kept happening in Israel that year, 1966,
that we could have talked for hours. Levi Eshkol had
formed a new cabinet, naming Abba Eban as foreign minister. There was a long strike at the Ashdod Port. Post
and telegraph charges had risen by 50%, so it was hard to
keep in touch with some of the family still back in Sana'a.

We were all thrilled that an Israeli, and a religious
Jew, had won the Nobel Prize for Literature. I had read
some of S.Y. Agnon's novels at school in my Literature
class, and my favorite book was "The Day Before Yester-
day". In his acceptance speech, he said that he had been
influenced by the Bible, the Mishna, the Talmud and the

Midrashim, and by Maimonides. What we liked was that
he also mentioned the influence of "every man, woman
and child I met in my life ..." It was also in this class that
I first began to write poetry to express my love for Jerusalem.

There were good things happening in Israel, and now
we all felt a part of them. We did not feel stigmatized as
our relatives had been when they first arrived from Yemen.
We even felt proud of the new Knesset building in Jerusalem, which had taken five years to build. Some of the men
were even discussing the American basketball star, Tal
Brody, who had come to live in Israel and was so inspiring
that basketball had become a very popular sport.

The new Knesset had been inaugurated in Jerusalem, and most of us had been to see it in Givat Ram. The
papers said it had cost 22 million lirot, a sum that was
beyond our comprehension.

I sat at a table talking to Dikla and her parents, Dina
and Yitzhak. They were my favorite cousins, and I didn't
see them often as it took several hours on the bus to reach
Rosh haAyin. Everyone thinks Israel such as tiny country, and by comparison with others I suppose it is, but if
you don't own a car and are religious, as we are, not travelling on the Sabbath, then you rarely get to see family in
other cities. My husband Kobi and I both worked six days
a week (he owns a small bookstore and I help him) so
although Mazal's yahrtzeit was hardly a happy occasion, it
did give us a chance to catch up on family news. We were
all drinking "gisher" and eating "malawah," for we kept
up many Yemenite traditions as far as food was concerned,
even if we'd long given up others. Another young cousin,
Doron, came to join us. He was 20 and had been in the
Army for two years. His family, Shalom's offspring, were
not scholars, but had worked in building for generations,
and my grandmother said that Doron had inherited their

physical strength. He looked very handsome in uniform with his broad shoulders and his sleeves rolled up to show muscular arms with strong biceps. Even though he and Dikla were distant cousins, I could see her looking at him with open admiration, and every now and again flipping her hair flirtatiously, as young girls tend to do.

"I have only ten more months and three weeks until my discharge" he told us. "Are you counting the hours too?" Dikla laughed. "And the minutes" he replied. "Enough is enough!"

Little did any of us know what the next year would bring.

Chapter 2

ON APRIL 7TH, THE telephone rang and Kobi seemed to be in shock. "What is it?" I asked, suddenly afraid. "One of the children....?" He shook his head. "Bracha, you'll have to handle the bookstore on your own for a while. I have to report to my unit. Syria opened fire on our tractors at Kibbutz Ha'on and now they're shelling the settlements."

Fear gripped my throat. I had only been a child of eight at the time of the 1948 War of Independence, but I could still recall the grief of families who had lost loved ones. And now my dear husband would be in danger.

I started to cry. "Kobi, don't go. You're over 30 now, you've done your part..."

He held me briefly. "I have to go home and find my uniform. Will the children be home yet?" Shira Mazal and Uri would have finished school, and the "metapelet" (nanny) would also have collected Moshe from his kindergarten. "I'm closing the store now. I'm coming home with you."

He nodded wordlessly. As soon as we got home, we turned on the radio. Dozens of houses had been demolished by Syrian fire east of Lake Kinneret, and an IDF officer had been killed. IAF jets had been sent to destroy the Syrian artillery batteries. There were dogfights taking place over Kibbutz Shamir.

The children bombarded their father with questions as he packed, watching uncomprehendingly as he put his "tallit" and "tefillin" in the bag.

"You will not be home tomorrow Abba? " Shira Mazal asked. "Where are you going?"

How do you explain war to a child? Kobi, anxious to get away, was very patient. "I have to go away for a while, to be a soldier," he told them. "I'll come back as soon as I can. You look after Imma and help her while I'm gone." Tears rolled down Moshele's cheeks. "It's going to be my birthday soon. I'll be five."

"I'll try to be back by then. It's still two weeks away. We'll have a little party. And if I can't get back, Imma will buy you a nice present."

"An ... an airplane," he insisted, between sobs. I smiled through my own tears. Kobi kissed us all and then was gone.

Over the next few days, even in the shop the radio was turned on and customers also wanted to hear the hourly bulletins. The Israel Air Force pursued the Syrian jets and downed six of them, two near Damascus. What would Egypt do, in reaction to Syria reporting that Israel was amassing forces on the northern border, which we denied?

President Nasser sent massive forces to the Sinai on May 14th. The shadow of war was again hovering over us, and I was desperately afraid, especially after Nasser closed the Tiran Straits to Israeli vessels. Russia was backing Egypt and there were intelligence reports that 80,000 troops were massed in the Sinai.

None of our soldiers were given leave, so we had to celebrate Moshe's birthday without his Abba. Money was tight because the bookstore only opened a few hours a day. I wanted to be home with the children and, in any case, there were few customers. The streets were almost empty.

I made a birthday cake and bought him a small aeroplane that he loved so much he took it to bed with him and cuddled it like a teddy bear. Two of his friends from kindergarten, Akiva and Ronni, came to the party and we sat around the table and sang "Yom huledet sameah – happy birthday to you" as he blew out the candles.

Shira Mazal and Uri had also bought him small gifts from their pocket money, a packet of crayons and a coloring book. For an hour I tried to be happy with the children, but kept hoping we might get a phone call from Abba. Of course it was impossible for him to call, and we didn't even know where he was.

Yitzhak Rabin hesitated about whether or not to declare war. David ben Gurion told him that he should not have called up the reserves and, by doing so, he had placed an isolated Israel in a very dangerous position. Rabin then called Major-General Ezer Weizman and offered to resign, and a doctor came and gave him a tranquilizer that made him sleep for 24 hours. The rumor of his collapse spread, and a national unity government was established, with Moshe Dayan appointed Defense Minister.

Two weeks later we were formally at war. On June 5th, 200 of our Air Force jets managed to destroy the air forces of Egypt, Syria and Jordan. There were 374 planes destroyed on the ground and the rest in dogfights. Israel had complete aerial supremacy during the six days of battle.

Kobi had only been home once. He had come for a Shabbat, but it was not like any other, and I felt more miserable than if I had been alone with the children. The Rabbis had given special permission for the radio to be left on for war bulletins, and he told me that if his phone rang, he would answer it and might have to leave.

Lunch on Shabbat was a farce. He made the blessings over the wine and bread, and I'd prepared one of our Yemenite foods he loved, "shaweeya," spicy meatballs with squash, and baked "saluf," our traditional pita bread. But even the children sensed that he had no patience to linger over the meal, or give a "Davar Torah" at their level so they could understand and ask questions. He craved sleep, but even with his eyes closed he was restless, as if poised for the phone call that would recall him to his unit.

I was a cauldron of mixed emotions. While I was glad to have him home, I resented that he was locked in a world I couldn't share. He was like a stranger, trying to be patient and affectionate, but not really with us. I found myself being sharp with the children and hating myself for it, while they looked strained and unhappy with the tension in the house, and the unaccustomed sound of the military radio station Galei Tzahal playing softly in the kitchen on Shabbat, giving news that frightened them without their fully understanding what was happening. I cried when it was time for him to leave, and this made the children even more insecure. Moshe clung to his pants' leg, even dropping his precious airplane in his efforts to prevent his father from leaving. Shira Mazal and Uri were quiet, not speaking to us nor to each other.

"I'll be back soon," he assured us. "We'll all be fine." He raced out to the jeep that was waiting for him, not even looking back.

The IDF entered Sinai in three columns, led by Yisrael Tal, Ariel Sharon and Avraham Yaffe. Kobi was with the latter that crossed the Egyptian border, advancing towards the rear of their forces. I heard that my young cousin Doron was with Sharon, storming the fortified zone of Abu-Agela, and I thought of Dikla and the way she had looked at him with so much admiration when we'd all been together at Mazal's tenth yahrtzeit.

I decided to call her in Rosh haAyin, and we tried to

comfort each other, she to reassure me that the war was going well, and I to tell her jokingly that Doron looked strong enough to take on the Syrians and the Egyptians single-handedly. Dikla was doing her "sherut leumi" (National Service) which was an option for religious girls who did not want to go in the Army. She worked in Rosh haAyin where she volunteered to help poor Yemenite families in many different ways, especially with children whose parents were often illiterate and who were struggling at school. "I think Doron really likes me," she confided. "We went out for coffee after the yahrtzeit get-together and we talked for hours. Maybe after the war, when he's out of the Army...," her voice trailed off. We couldn't think that far ahead. We were all living from one news bulletin to the next. It was impossible to make any plans.

The next morning, we experienced war first-hand when Jerusalem was attacked. We huddled in bomb shelters while Jordan attacked us, firing artillery day and night. We were terrified, and heard on the radio that Syrian jets had raided Haifa Bay and the northern settlements.

The next day, June 6th, a miracle happened. Our troops moved forward throughout the whole of Samaria, conquering Latrun, Jenin, Kalkilya and Ramallah; while Moshe Dayan ordered the Paratroopers' Brigade, under the command of "Motta" Gur, to conquer Jerusalem's Old City. They conquered most of the Arab villages around the city, and fought fierce battles in the bunkers on Ammunition Hill, where we suffered heavy losses.

We were expecting America to come to our aid, but all President Johnson did was to condemn the war, citing it "needless and destructive." He thought it could be ended through the United Nations Security Council, and of course we got no help from the British. As Kobi and my parents had always maintained, we had only ourselves to depend on and the protection of the Almighty. We would always be "a nation that stands alone."

The Mayor of Jerusalem, Teddy Kollek, tried to boost our morale. He acknowledged that our homes had become a battleground, but said that all of our citizens, rich and poor, veteran and new immigrant, children and adults, were standing steadfast. He praised our courage under fire, and promised that the damage would be repaired, and the city rebuilt to be more beautiful and treasured than ever.

The truth was that it was only necessity that kept me brave. I couldn't show the children that I was afraid, not only for their father who was away fighting in the south, but I was also scared of our own danger. We took a risk each time we left home and we saw the damage the Jordanians were causing, many houses reduced to piles of rubble; many families burying their dead or visiting the wounded in overcrowded hospitals. I was proud of the two older children, the way they would play with Moshe and distract him from the real fear that walked our streets. Ten people had already been killed in Jerusalem and one hundred wounded. Our hot and cramped bomb shelters were places we dreaded.

Every day brought new revelations that our prayers were being answered. It wasn't as bad as our War of Independence in 1948 when the city was on starvation rations and almost without water for weeks. This time we were not afraid that Jewish Jerusalem might fall, as the Jewish Quarter had fallen. That had broken our matriarch Mazal's heart, when all of her dreams had been shattered, and she was carried bodily out of her beloved store "The Pomegranate Pendant" just before the Arabs looted it and burnt it to the ground. The Jordanians' shelling this time was almost aimless. It seemed more like obedience to Nasser's order for a diversion that would cause Israeli forces to leave Sinai so they could protect the capital.

On the morning of June 7th, a miracle happened. At 10 a.m., the paratroopers broke through Lions' Gate and liberated the Western Wall, Judaism's holiest site. The Temple Mount commander, Motta Gur, stood near the Wall with his officers and announced on the radio in emotional tones: "The Temple Mount is in our hands!" After hours of fierce battles, the sweaty and weary paratroopers burst into tears. The chief military Rabbi, Shlomo Goren, arrived at the *Kotel* (Western Wall) and blew triumphant blasts on the *shofar* (ram's horn). He prayed: "This is the day we have been yearning for. Let us rejoice in it."

Chapter 3

ALL OUR PRAYERS SEEMED to be answered. Only a day later, on June 8th, it was clear that the Egyptian army had crumbled. Our forces advanced quickly to the Western Sinai, seizing Egyptian Army bases and airfields. We were told that thousands of Egyptian soldiers were left in the desert, separated from their units, and were begging for food and water. At the end of the day, on the fourth day of the war, we reached the Suez Canal. The conquest of the Sinai Peninsula was completed.

The next day, the action shifted to an offensive against the Syrian troops on the Golan. Soon their fortified posts which had been terrorizing our settlements below, were captured. Tragically, our losses of brave men were very heavy. No names were released at this time as relatives had first to be notified, and because none of us knew exactly where our husbands and sons had been sent, it was a time of terrible anxiety for those who had men fighting, which meant almost every family in Israel. Planes kept arriving at Lydda Airport filled with returning Israelis, lining up at a special army desk, to receive their call-up notices on the spot. They may have left years earlier for easier lives abroad ... more money, more leisure, no reserve duty, or "miluim" as they called it, but when they knew their homeland was threatened, all these considerations paled into insignificance. As well as the fear and anxiety, there was a heart-warming feeling of family as we all bonded together against a common enemy. We were all Jews, all Israelis, whether we were religious or secular, voted Likud or Labor, wore "kippot" or went bare-headed. There were no more strangers. We were all family.

The Northern Command was headed by Major-General David Elazar, known to all as "Dado." No matter how high a rank, most important personalities (like "Motta" Mordechai Gur) were given pet names in Israel. It not only humanized them, it made them part of "us." The IDF stormed Kuneitra, and Damascus Radio announced that the city had fallen, even before our troops reached it, so that the UN Security Council would impose a cease-fire. This caused the Syrian residents to flee. The cease-fire was enforced at 4.30 p.m. The Golan Heights had been captured. The Six-Day War had ended.

"How beautiful upon the mountains are the feet of the messenger of good tidings that announces peace!", we are told in the Bible. Even back in 1821, Rav Nachman of Bratslav wrote that "Jerusalem will be rebuilt only through peace" and those of us who lived here hugged each other and wept with joy. All day the radio played Naomi Shemer's song: "Jerusalem of Gold – Yerushalayim shel Zahav." Performed by Shuli Nathan, it became an instant hit. She wrote it as a song of longing and nostalgia, but now it was a victory anthem that was sung by the paratroopers who had conquered the Old City. She also added two verses in honor of the reality and performed them for the soldiers in al-Arish: "We're back to the water cisterns, to the market and the square. A shofar sounds on the Temple Mount in the Old City."

Kobi finally came home for Shavuot, when we celebrate receiving the Ten Commandments. It was only seven weeks after Passover, but that seemed far away, in another life. Shira Mazal had learned at school the special meanings in Judaism of the number seven. Her teacher had told the class that according to legend, seven things were created two thousand years before the Creation. There are seven heavens; seven kinds of dwellers in Paradise; a good man is clothed in seven garments of glorious clouds before he enters the Gates of Heaven; the cock crows seven times each night to call the lazy ones to waken, thus giving them seven warnings that he who loves sleep must learn to love poverty. Man's life is divided into seven stages: infancy, childhood, boyhood, young manhood, prime of manhood, middle age and old age. The seven branches of the candelabra represent the seven days of the week, and also the seven great planets of the universe that the ancients knew about. Even more important is seven times seven... the number of days that passed from the time the Almighty freed the Jews from slavery in Egypt, to when He made them free men forever through the Ten Commandments, which is why we celebrate Shavuot.

If only all the people of the earth would abide by them, we could rid the world of evil ... no theft, no murder or heart-breaking wars; no adultery; no lies; no envy; no idolatry; no slavery.

But even in the imperfect world, this Shavuot we had much to celebrate. Kobi and I, Shira Mazal, Uri and Moshe joined 250,000 Jews in a united and liberated Jerusalem. Although a temporary order banned it, we joined the throng climbing the new road to Mount Zion, walked down the stairs near the city walls, passed through the Dung Gate and reached the Kotel. This was the last time we would refer to it as "the Wailing Wall"... it would be the Western Wall. We all wept, hugged each other and kissed the stones. We also placed notes in the cracks, with our petitions. They say the "Shechina", the Holy Presence, has never left this last remaining Wall of the

Temple. We all put in a note. Mine prayed that Israel would never again be attacked, but that we could live in peace and prosperity for all the generations to come. Even little Moshe, who couldn't write yet insisted I put in a note for him. "Tell G-d I want a bike," he instructed me sternly.

We hoped to return to normal life as quickly as possible, but somehow we couldn't. During the war, while the men were away fighting, women had rallied amazingly, driving buses, filling sandbags, doing whatever was needed as volunteers in the hospitals. We had quickly cleaned out the storerooms in our buildings, to convert them to bomb shelters, and many streets were littered with old discarded rickety furniture waiting for garbage trucks to take them away.

Our Egged buses, that had been co-opted into war service, returned to our streets, giving a semblance of normalcy. But there were wounded in all the hospitals. There were bereaved families, whose lives could never again be the same. There were shattered buildings in need of repair. There was once-divided Jerusalem that somehow had to be unified. Barbed wire and mine fields still had to be removed.

Physical damage can be repaired slowly and painstakingly. Psychological and emotional damage can take longer. Kobi was home with us in body, but the gentle, nurturing husband and father we had known just weeks before, had undergone a major transition. He was depressed but didn't want to talk about it. He was preoccupied and seemed to have lost interest in everything. Our bookshop, which he had run so enthusiastically, now seemed to be just a necessary chore. When the children wanted to share the highlights of their day with him, he would listen patiently, but he was abstracted and they soon gave up. Israel was celebrating a miraculous victory, but I felt that I had somehow lost a major battle.

Women At The Western Wall

It is barely dawn in Jerusalem
And yet, even now, the Kotel is not alone.

By my side, there are three other women...
Two are swaying devoutly,
Eyes closed, muttering petitions fiercely,
Demandingly –
Old ladies whose patience with God has run out.

A young girl looks incongruous
In jeans and sneakers,
She seems unsure of what to do, what to say,
So she stands immobile
While her eyes do the pleading
And a single tear courses down her cheek.
I think she is the one
Whose petition will be answered,
She seems to need a blessing
So very much ...

From the men's side you can hear
The formal *davening* of *Shachrit*,
But the words were written by others.

We four women have no ritual,
We each talk one-to-one with the Creator.

Our hands press the cold stones
For we know the benison of touch.

In the background, a church bell is tolling;
The *muezzin* calls the Moslems to prayer.
We lack these accoutrements,
We just touch the Wall
As ages of sadness flood our being.

They say God's presence has never departed,
So we say our prayers,
Our pleas, and our petitions,
In a hush of silence.

We raise our eyes
As a weak sun
Breaks through Jerusalem's dawn.

Four women praying
Each in her own fashion
For blessings
That no man could ever comprehend.

Chapter 4

THE CHILDREN WERE IN bed. We had eaten supper, but Kobi had just pushed the food around on his plate.

"Kobi, we have to talk."

"There's nothing to talk about."

"Yes there is," I insisted. "What's wrong with you?"

"You wouldn't understand."

"Try me. Please don't keep shutting me out."

He was silent for a few minutes. "I can't just pretend the war never happened. You'd think six days is such a short time, and there were just a few weeks I was in the army leading up to it. Yet I experienced things that haunt me, that I'll never forget. Friends I joked with and fought with were killed in front of my eyes. I couldn't save them. They were still young men, like me. Husbands, fathers, sons, brothers. We won – but what a price we had to pay!" He began to cry. I'd never seen him cry before and I felt so impotent.

"Maybe we could get you some help," I stammered. "Some counselling. Or tablets against depression. I remember reading an article …"

"If I'm depressed, Bracha, it's because I have reason to be. It's not just a figment of my imagination. No kind words or tranquilizers can change the reality."

He was right. Probably the only ones who could understand what he was feeling were comrades who had shared the same experience. But the old cliché that time heals has a lot of truth in it. I still sensed an underlying sadness in my husband as the days passed, but there were other days when the children made him laugh, when we recaptured the loving intimacy we had known, when customers engaged him in lively conversation and when he made a conscious effort to brighten up the atmosphere. Business had improved as the border between Old and New Jerusalem had been abolished. The Army had relinquished control to the civilian police, and the curfew in the Old City had been lifted.

One evening, Kobi said to me: "Bracha, I want you to invite all your family over."

"You're joking," I said. "We are living all over the country. And in our small apartment, where would I put everyone?"

"It's summer, and the school holidays," he reminded me. "We could make a picnic in the Jerusalem Forest."

"But what for? Why would we want to do that?"

"I have a proposition to make. I want to discuss it with everyone. Especially with your great-aunt Ruchama, and great-uncles Assaf and Shalom and all their children."

"Can't you tell me?" I asked petulantly.

"It's a surprise. I want to find out first if it's feasible."

No amount of coaxing would make him say more. I contacted all the relatives, and just as they had for Mazal's yahrtzeit, they agreed to take a day off for this mysterious get-together.

It was a glorious summer day, warm and perfumed like the taste of rich kiddush wine. We met at a designated spot in the Jerusalem Forest where there were wooden benches and tables. Some had brought small portable "mangals" or barbecues on which they were roasting meat that sent out delectable odors. Others had brought sandwiches, fruit and thermos flasks of gisher or tea. The children were laughing with delight on the slides and swings of the adjacent playground.

After everyone had eaten and drunk their fill, and the children were playing nearby, the small ones asleep on blankets, Kobi outlined his idea. I was as shocked as everyone else.

"I want to know what you think of my idea," he began. "On many occasions I've heard you all talk about Mazal's wonderful store "The Pomegranate Pendant." Now that the Old City is again ours, and we still have the deeds to her properties, why don't we pool our resources, and rebuild it and open it once again for the tourists who will be flocking here from all over the world."

There was a gasp of astonishment, with mine perhaps the loudest of all.

Chapter 5

OF COURSE THERE WAS a barrage of opposition. Shalom said sadly, "My mother wanted the name to die with her." Assaf corrected him. "No, she didn't want the name used unless it could be rebuilt the same way in the same location."

Ruchama said wonderingly: "But we have no silversmiths in the family now. Our parents and Djeddi, they were the ones who knew how to create the beautiful jewelry."

"That's not quite true," came a voice from the back. Miriam, the daughter of Mazal's sister Shoshanna, stood up. "My daughter Orpah has studied at Bezalel Art School, and jewelry design was her main interest. Tell them about it." She nudged her daughter, a shy girl we had hardly noticed at our family get-togethers.

Orpah stood up slowly, next to her mother. Her long black hair almost fell in a curtain, obscuring half her face, but her olive skin, dark eyes and slender figure showed her to be a true Yemenite.

"I spent a lot of time studying Yemenite jewelry and have made lots of filigree necklaces and earrings," she admitted. "One piece is even on display at the Israel Museum, in the Ethnography Department." She fingered her own necklace, which we craned to look at. It was a "hamsah," a tiny pendant in the shape of an open hand, that Oriental Jews wear as a talisman to ward off the Evil Eye. Small as it was, we could see how beautifully it was wrought in silver filigree with a tiny pearl at its center.

"It is beautiful," we all agreed. "But could you make enough to fill a store, and keep up the supply?" was Kobi's practical question.

"No, I would need help. But our family knows some Yemenite jewellers who still practice their trade. They could also supply us."

"We didn't only sell jewelry," Ruchama reminded us. "There was Yfat's wonderful embroidery too." Yfat and Yitzhak, Mazal's close friends from Sana'a, had long passed on, but their son Evyatar's wife and daughter Dganit still sold their unique, scrolled embroidery to the business called "Gargush" which some of the family now ran in New Jerusalem.

"And there were tefillin and mezuzot for the doorposts, and all kinds of ritual items," Assaf added excitedly. "Kobi, you could supply the books."

Suddenly, everyone was talking and contributing ideas. Kobi sat there, looking happy in a way I hadn't seen since before the war. Tirza still crocheted baby clothes; Yfat's daughters-in-law and granddaughters embroidered challah (bread) covers and head scarves; Assaf's grandsons were "sofers" (scribes); some of Shalom's family who were still in the building trade, said they would love to be involved in the rebuilding, especially as Shalom could remember every detail of how the store had looked.

What had seemed like an impossible dream was perhaps to become a reality. It was an exciting idea, and I felt proud that my husband Kobi, who had no blood connection to Mazal and the ben-Yichya family, had been the one to think of it. I could imagine Mazal, Ezra and Djeddi looking down from heaven and giving us their blessing.

Chapter 6

OF COURSE IT DIDN'T happen immediately. It meant a big upheaval in all our lives, and dealing with the Israeli bureaucracy put us all on the brink of a nervous breakdown. But eventually we got permission to rebuild the store, and Mazal's old home in the Chosh was given back to our family. It was situated just west of the north end of Chabad Street, adjacent to what had been the Sukkat Shalom Courtyard of Rabbi Yeshaya Bardaki. There were three rooms above a broad, ivy-covered staircase and a garden below. It was neglected, but there was no real structural damage and Shalom said it could easily be restored. In the garden, the carob tree and the orange tree amazingly still grew, and I remembered how much Mazal had loved them, especially when the orange blossoms perfumed the air with sweetness.

We had another family get-together to discuss who would live there. Of course it was offered first to Ruchama, Assaf and Shalom, but they all said they were too old to start again in the Old City. So much building and reconstruction would be taking place in the Rova, the Jewish Quarter, and there would be noise and dust all day long, probably for months to come. Assaf was planning soon to enter a nursing home, and Ruchama and Shalom were also old and had become frail in recent years. "I would love to live there," I offered tentatively. "We're only a family of five, we could manage." I looked at Kobi, fearing I should have consulted him first, but he was smiling.

When no one else said they wanted it, Ruchama held her hand out to me. "It is fitting that your daughter, Shira Mazal, should live there. I hope it will be a home of happiness and peace for you."

I could barely contain my excitement as the family left, but then I noticed Dikla sitting alone by the window. I went over to her. "You look so sad. What's the matter? Did you want it?"

"Oh no." She gave a laugh that had no happiness in it, only a kind of bitterness. "Why would I need it? I'll never marry and have a family."

"What are you talking about?"

A single tear coursed down her cheek. "I thought that when the war was over, Doron and I would get together. I made a fool of myself. He didn't want me."

I searched for words. "Well, you are distant cousins. Maybe that's the reason…"

"He loves someone else. He said he is very fond of me, but just like a sister. He apologized for giving the wrong impression, but it wasn't his fault. I was stupid!"

"You're not stupid," I said gently. "You're a lovely, intelligent young lady, and you're only twenty. Your life is just beginning. "When you finish your "sherut leumi," I'm sure you'll go to university and meet lots of potential suitors. Or I know a lady, a match-maker…."

She shook her head. "That's the last thing I want. If I can't have Doron, I don't want anybody. Not now. Not ever."

Chapter 7

I SPOKE TO DIKLA several times by telephone over the next few weeks. At first she sounded lethargic, just going through the motions of her daily routine. But after a while, she had news to tell me of progress she was making in her work in Rosh haAyin ... an illiterate Yemenite woman, married at age 13, who was starting to read and, as a result, had higher self-esteem and had earned much more respect from her husband and children; a street gang that she had persuaded to help clean up the litter in their town, instead of just "hanging out" in the evenings, bored and usually engaged on the edge of criminal activities. Her voice had brightened, and even though she never mentioned Doron, she seemed to be finding happiness in her accomplishments with the Yemenite community in the development town where she was working.

I didn't have too much time to think about Dikla and her problems. There were family meetings all the time as our old-new store "The Pomegranate Pendant" was being rebuilt, and excitement building up as to what would be displayed and by whom; if we would re-create the showroom where Djeddi used to work so that a curious public could watch the artisans as they created their wares; and who would be the sales staff, buyers, administrators etc. There were endless discussions, a few arguments, but on the whole it boded well for a successful enterprise.

However, no one lives in a vacuum, and the rest of Israel was not focused on our activities. The war may have been officially over, but it seemed our country was never to enjoy peace. Five Egyptian planes had been downed, with two of our Israeli aircraft lost. Our jets had bombed Egyptian missile and artillery bases across the Suez Canal in response to increased Egyptian shelling and commando raids. Although we lost two planes, the pilots were able to bail out in Israeli territory and were saved. The operation was intended to give the Egyptian High Command second thoughts about its plans for an early attack on Israel.

However, despite its trouncing, Egypt claimed to its people that its anti-aircraft guns had downed 17 of our planes in battles over the Suez Canal and Sinai. They said it was "their greatest victory" since the Six-Day War, and did not mention their losses. Continuing their usual fantasy propaganda, they claimed they were capable of achieving "victory over the enemy, whether they were on the defensive or offensive." Luckily, no Israeli took them seriously, but we could never relax. Their recent humiliation had caused them again to bluster, so that there was never a chance to relax our watchfulness.

Exciting things were also happening outside of Israel. Two American astronauts, Neil Armstrong and Edwin Aldrin, had made a dream come true. They stepped on to the moon's surface from their space-ship "The Eagle" which landed on the moon's "Sea of Tranquillity", after a dangerous descent from the Apollo II command ship. It was man's first visit to another planet.

With such world-shattering events taking place, the concerns of our tiny country probably paled into insignificance on an international level. But it has never been like that for our people. Because we are one small family, we celebrate together and we grieve together. Whenever one of our soldiers is killed or wounded, any of our citizens attacked by terrorists, we all feel it. We watch funerals on television of young people we have never met, yet we weep as if they were our own children. In calm times we may all fight about politics and religion, but there is a fierce love for each other, that unites us in a bond that no one outside of our country has ever been able to understand.

Chapter 8

I HAVE HEARD THAT in Western countries, politics are just on the edge of peoples' consciences, and they are much more concerned about education, the economy, planning holidays, moving up the ladder of success, and acquiring all kinds of luxuries. There are many materialists among our people too, but the main focus of our attention is always the security situation. Especially if we have sons and daughters entering their teen years, we know that joining the army is ever looming closer. At 18, most Western youth are leaving home to attend college, sowing some wild oats as they sample their first taste of unsupervised freedom, with all the fun and excitement that goes with such heady years. Our youngsters, on the contrary, are being interviewed by the IDF, donning uniforms, undergoing basic training and taking on responsibilities far beyond their years. Each birthday, while pretending to celebrate, parents are mentally ticking off how many more years they will have them safely at home.

Egypt is conducting a war of attrition against Israel. Our Prime Minister, Levi Eshkol has died and Golda Meir has become Prime Minister, a great victory for the feminists amongst us. With enemies on every border, Israel can never let down its defences and five French-built missile boats, which we purchased, have been smuggled out of Cherbourg harbor in defiance of the French embargo. They have already arrived here.

My own life has become very exciting. Mazal's old apartment in the Chosh had needed very little refurbishing, and Shalom's grandsons have done a wonderful job. We have moved in and I feel Mazal's presence still even though so many years have passed since she lived here. When I climb up to the roof, I can see the whole area around the Temple Mount, just as Mazal would have seen it. I could imagine crowds of pilgrims gathering there at the three Festivals, bringing their sacrifices to the Holy Temple. I feel humble and deeply privileged as I look at the sweeping panorama of domed roofs and towers, dusty alleys and broad boulevards. It is heart-warming now that we have the Old City back again to see crowds of Jews, locals and tourists, shopping, strolling and praying at the Western Wall after having been denied access to it for so many years.

The roofs of the Rova, the Jewish Quarter, are knobbly white domes, while the Christian Quarter favors red brick tiles. My new apartment is at the top of a flight of stairs, but below I have access to the garden that Mazal had loved so much, with its sweet-smelling orange tree. Although I am not doing it consciously, I find that the memory of this remarkable woman is influencing the way I feel about so many things. When I furnished the three rooms, I pictured in my mind's eye the way she would have done it, and I consulted often with my great-aunt and uncles who had once lived here.

Ruchama gave me a beautiful watercolor she had painted as a gift for her mother when she was young, many decades ago, before glaucoma had almost claimed her vision. It was the skyline of the Old City at twilight, as the indigo shadows lengthened and the sky began to be strewn with stars, like diamonds scattered randomly on blue velvet. I hung it in the entrance hall, so that it is the first thing you see as you enter the apartment. On another wall in the "salon," I have created a feature of different kinds of "hamsahs" that Yemenites and Oriental Jews be-lieve are talismans against the "Evil Eye". In deference to Mazal's memory, I painted the outside walls blue, as Assaf told me his mother had once done. She believed that any evil spirits that might come would be confused when they came to get us, and think it was the sky, so they would leave. Kobi laughed at me, but deep-down he also had great respect for our Yemenite traditions and he was so excited at the prospect of re-opening "The Pomegranate Pendant" that I had almost free reign in anything I wanted to do in our home.

One morning I woke up with the remnants of a dream tugging at my consciousness. I tried to recapture it, but it eluded me all the morning although I knew it had some-thing to do with Mazal. When I went into the garden to pick some of the oranges from the tree and to collect car-obs that had fallen to the ground, I began to remember. The dream had been about herbs, and it seemed to me that Mazal wanted me to plant them, just as she had done, and to use them not only to flavor our food, but also for healing.

The idea excited me. I'd never had a garden before, so I didn't know where to start. My great-aunt Ruchama seemed to have the strongest memories of her mother's daily life in this house, so I went to visit her. "Bracha my dear," she informed me, "it's true that she learned all about herbs from her own mother before she left Sana'a, and she planted them in Israel, but she stopped relying on them for healing after her dear husband, my father, passed away. Before then, she thought she could use them for healing and had no need of modern medicine. But in the face of such a disease as typhoid, they were impotent, and also when I found that I was going blind from glaucoma before my wedding, she no longer talked about their special properties."

"But she continued to grow them?"

Ruchama nodded. "It was hard for her to give up something she had learned from her mother. Tradition was so important to her. She taught me what she knew, but always with a warning that with serious illness one must consult a doctor."

More of the dream came back to me and I could almost feel her hand on mine planting the tiny seedlings in the holy earth of Eretz Israel. Ruchama was very patient with me. With half-closed eyes, she tried to recapture some of her mother's words.

"I remember Imma telling me that you always steep, but never boil , herbs. You bring a cup of water to the boil, then turn the fire off. Put a spoonful of herbs like melissa in it and let it stand for 20 minutes. This is steeping. Then you strain it and drink it an hour before your meal, or before you retire. If it's too strong, put less herbs in the cup." She smiled as she saw me taking notes. "Roots must be simmered for at least 30 minutes to extract their medicinal value, but flowers and leaves should not be boiled. Just steep them as I described."

We made a list of the herbs I should purchase at a plant nursery she remembered. Basil, called "reichan", was the first with its aromatic leaves that could be dried and crushed to help you breathe more easily, or to cure a headache and reduce a fever. The leaves could also be soaked in wine to make a tonic. She talked of "hel" – cardamon and "chasa el-ban" or rosemary, to strengthen the memory and the heart. Chives to lower blood pressure. Sweet marjoram to heal infections. Sage is good to cure coughs and peppermint or "nana" helps the digestion. Some came with warnings. "Mother always ate two leaves a day of Gotu Kola or Indian Pennywort. It's supposed to give you long life … indeed she lived well into her 90s, but she said if you ate too much it was a narcotic that could make you dizzy and even put you in a coma. Lavender and lemon verbena make a wonderful perfumed tea, and both camomile and melissa tea give you sweet dreams…"

I had almost filled a notebook when I left her. I drove straight to the plant nursery that specialized in herbs and filled the back seat with tiny seedlings in small plastic containers that had once been filled with yoghurt or leben. The owner of the nursery had given me more advice on how to space them and how often to water them, which herbs needed shade and which sunlight. By the time I reached home I was filled with excitement. The garden was not really mine, but common property also for the two other apartments in the building, so I had to ask my neighbors' permission. They were more than happy to have me take over the gardening, so I chose a quiet corner that had very little growing there, squatted down and, with trowel and gardening gloves, began to create the beautiful, fragrant herb garden that all of my family would come to know forever after as "Mazal's Corner."

Chapter 9

THE HEBREW MONTH OF Adar had arrived, and with it, the first signs of Spring. March is a lovely season in Israel, although there can still be cold and rainy days, sometimes even snow in Jerusalem. But this year, interspersed with strong, cold winds, there were days of pure sunshine when the sky was blue and cloudless, the air perfumed by the first almond blossom, jonquils and anemones. Days such as these create so much inspiration for writing my poetry. Little red poppies and even a few creamy and mauve cyclamens dotted the grass, and my herbs had grown tall enough for me to begin picking some of the leaves. The chives gave a lovely onion flavor to our salads and we finished heavier meals with a cup of mint tea to aid the digestion.

In two weeks it would be Purim. Although our family had let some of the Yemenite traditions lapse over the years, we always enjoyed re-creating them at Purim. My great-aunt Ruchama and uncles Assaf and Shalom could still remember their grandfather Djeddi sitting on a carpet chanting Oriental songs and smoking his "nargilla," a long water pipe. They said that at Purim they always ate fresh, sweet dishes made from dates and figs, in contrast to their usual spiced food. Young girls wore silver rings and danced, shaking their tambourines, known in Israel as "tof Miriam" because of Moses' sister Miriam, who had sung to their accompaniment after the parting of the Red Sea.

This was the costume Shira Mazal donned for Purim but her younger brothers, Uri and Moshe, wanted less imaginative costumes like their friends. Uri decided to dress like a policeman and Moshe as a pirate. I suppose that with each successive generation born in Israel, traditions become more diluted. It is inevitable, but we tried, Kobi and I, to remind the children every now and again, of the Yemenite roots from which they had sprung.

We made up "mishloach manot," gifts of prepared foods that the children delivered to friends and neighbors, and were the recipients of quite a few in return. The kids were thrilled with the sweets, chocolates, nuts, cakes and small bottles of wine and grape juice that now adorned our table. It was a school holiday, so they were in and out every hour, breathless with excitement.

The day was almost drawing to a close when the telephone rang. It was Dikla.

"I'm in Jerusalem. May I call in later this evening? I've made you a nice "mishloach manot"… cakes and cookies that I baked myself. I'm afraid Purim will be over, but it's never too late to do a "mitzvah" is it?

"Of course not. You sound very happy. Have you been enjoying yourself today?"

"Not just today. For a few weeks already."

"What do you mean?"

"Well, I have a new friend."

"By all means bring her with you."

"Actually Bracha, it's a guy."

I smiled to myself. This was Dikla who was never going to want anyone except Doron, who would remain single for her whole life. How much time had elapsed since those words … maybe four months?

"What's his name?"

"Menelik Bogale."

"That's a strange name. I guess he's not Yemenite?" I couldn't help the remark. It was almost a conditioned reflex in our family, but we always hoped that new partners would share our culture and tradition, even though we were now so assimilated into the general population.

"No, he's not Yemenite. Do you mind, Bracha?"

"Of course not," I said emphatically, trying to disguise my disappointment. "I'm delighted that you sound so happy." That at least was true. "Tell me about him. Where is he from?"

"You'll meet him later. Then you can ask him whatever you want."

I knew we were in for a surprise, but could never have anticipated that it would shake us to our very foundations.

Chapter 10

IT WAS QUITE LATE when the doorbell rang. The children were already asleep, exhausted from their day of fancy dress parades, and all the unaccustomed chocolate and cake they had consumed. Kobi and I had also over-indulged in food at the Purim "seudah" and had a few drinks in the custom of the holiday. I was sleepy and a bit annoyed that they had arrived so late, but prepared a beaming smile to greet Dikla and her mysterious friend.

I didn't see him at first when I opened the door, as Dikla was carrying a big basket full of wonderful things to eat. Even under the cellophane and ribbons I could make out cakes and chocolates, fruit and a bottle of wine. I kissed her warmly, and then he moved into the light.

He was a good-looking young man, I guessed about 24 years of age. He was only slightly taller than Dikla, with close-cropped curly hair and big brown eyes. What rooted me to the spot was that he was black, not dark-skinned like a Yemenite, but totally, completely black.

He smiled widely, showing beautiful pearly-white teeth. "May I come in Bracha?"

"Of course, of course," I stammered, barely able to move aside.

He laughed. "You're surprised, no?"

"Well yes. I mean – you're Ethiopian. Yes … a Falasha,

a Cushi … is that what you're called?"

Dikla corrected me. "He is from Beta Israel," she said gently. "Falasha is an insulting term meaning 'stranger.' Ethiopia is sometimes referred to as Cush, but he is one of the ancient, once-lost but newly-discovered Jews of Beta Israel."

I was in such shock that Kobi took over from me, warmly shaking his hand and showing him to a seat. I went into the kitchen to prepare coffee and refreshments, and Dikla followed me.

"Bracha, I should have prepared you. I thought it might surprise you, but you can't deal with it, can you?" she said sadly.

"I just need to get used to the idea," I said defensively.

"And if he'd been Ashkenazi or Sephardi?"

"It would have been easier," I admitted.

"I didn't think you would be a racist, like my parents," she said slowly. "They won't even talk to me."

"Oh, I'm not," I hastened to reassure her. "I'm sure he's a good Jew, a good man…"

She sat on a stool near the stove. "He's a wonderful human being, one of the kindest people I have ever met. We work together in Rosh haAyin. He's a qualified social worker and helps everyone, not just Beta Israel. And I love him," she added, tears sliding down her cheeks.

I put my arms around her. "I'll help you with your parents," I promised. I had never thought of myself as a racist and the idea that I might be horrified me. But we had our own Yemenite culture and roots. Dina and Yitzhak were my favorite cousins and in their immediate family several members had not married Yemenites without it traumatizing them. Yet in some way this was different. We knew almost nothing about the Beta Israel or their history, language and beliefs, their interpretation of Judaism. We all feel uneasy when faced with a culture that is totally foreign to us. I would try to convince Dina and Yitzhak that it could be a successful union. But first I had to convince myself!

Next Year In Jerusalem

Until now
It was just a name...
Turned into a prayer.

Part of our liturgies, it has been solemnly
intoned:
Next year in Jerusalem.

But "next year" meant something else,
Nebulous, indefinite...

For their children...
Not for us.

Until now
It was just an image:
Minarets, spires and domes
Dreaming into the mist
Of Biblical Jerusalem.

But it was a vision,
A fantasy conjured by the mind
From childhood stories
In ancient books...
Not really there.
...Until now

They dwelt and prophesied
In Old Jerusalem.
But then they came...

And the dream
Has become the Jewish people's reality...

We are in Jerusalem.

Chapter 11

WHEN WE CAME BACK into the salon with the re-freshments, Kobi was telling Menelik a joke. "... So these two Ethiopians saw this Yemenite girl, and one said to the other: 'Take a look at the blondini!'"

"Kobi!" I said aghast. It was a joke in the worst possible taste in the circumstances, but Menelik had thrown his head back and was laughing uproariously.

"It's O.K.," he reassured me, "It's very funny."

Even Dikla was smiling, but I still felt embarrassed. "Look," he said to me, "Bracha, I'm black. I know it's still a curiosity in Israel, and a few people have said some very hurtful things. But as more of the Beta Israel reach Israel, we'll be less of a rarity and after a while, we'll be accepted just as the Russians were when they first came."

He was right. I remembered the first Russian "olim" and how they stood out, especially little girls who wore big bows of brightly-colored ribbons in their hair. Now they dressed the same as everyone else, and except for their accent which they would eventually probably lose in one generation, they were indistinguishable from the other children.

Kobi and Menelik seemed to have slipped into an easy camaraderie and gradually I began to relax.

"Geographically," Menelik was explaining, "Ethiopia

and Yemen are almost neighbors, with just the Red Sea dividing us. We believe that once there were over half a million of us, Beta Israel, the House of Israel. A century ago, we were 200,000, but today our number is estimated to be 32,000. We dreamt of Zion for our twenty centuries in exile. We held onto the same Book, our Amharic language and Jewish laws as we understood them, all that time. The older name for Ethiopia was Abyssinia, or Cush as the Bible has it. We Jews were there long before the 4th century when Christianity came there, and we ourselves are unsure where we came from... We may have wandered to Ethiopia from Egypt, Southern Arabia, even Yemen. I think we came from Israel as one of the ten lost Tribes, the Tribe of Dan."

"What part of Ethiopia did you come from?" I asked.

"The source of the Nile, Lake Tana area in the northwest is where the majority of Beta Israel settled. There are hundreds of Jewish villages located there. But I went to a Jewish school in Addis Ababa."

Dikla interjected: "Haven't you noticed that there is a similarity of character between Beta Israel and we Yemenites? Both people are recognized as gentle and refined."

"I don't really know any other Ethiopians, I mean Beta Israel," I admitted, blushing.

"Isaiah prophesied that we would come back. He wrote: 'And it shall come to pass in that day that the Lord will set His hand again a second time to recover the remnant of His people that shall remain, from Abyssinia and from Egypt, and from Pathros, and from Cush...'" quoted Menelik. "The Chief Rabbi, David ibn Zimra, ruled in 16th century Cairo that those 'from the land of Cush' are without doubt the Tribe of Dan of the seed of Israel. And the Israeli Sephardi Chief Rabbi, Ovadia Yosef, has now confirmed this ruling."

"Are all your family here?" asked Kobi.

"No, my parents have not been so lucky. They are still waiting, just as one brother and two sisters are. But I have another brother and sister and their families living in Ashkelon, and some cousins in Afula."

"Why were you named Menelik?" I asked.

He smiled. "You have heard of King Solomon and the Queen of Sheba, another name for Ethiopia. Well, the Bible tells us in First Kings, Chapter 10, that when the Queen of Sheba came to Jerusalem, King Solomon gave her 'all her desire.' It seems that some of what she desired resulted in a son, named Menelik, the founder of a royal dynasty. In fact, the Emperor, Haile Selassie, known as 'The Lion of Judah,' eventually came from this union also."

Dikla added: "The Queen gave Solomon 120 talents of gold, a great store of spices and precious jewels. It was a real love story."

I had many more questions, but I felt it would be rude to keep asking. One thing had been accomplished though. I would have no trouble in putting Dikla's case to her parents, for with every minute that passed, I was filled with admiration for this charming young man with his deference to us, his obvious respect and affection for our young kinswoman, and his love of Torah. It must have been a heroic task for him to integrate into Israeli society, to master Hebrew, to serve in the Army and to educate and support himself as he had obviously done.

As a teenager I had received a gift from a school-friend, a record from the 1950s of an American musical called "South Pacific." I remember some of the lyrics from one of the songs:

"You have to be taught
    Before it's too late

To hate all the people
Your relatives hate;
Before you are six, or seven, or eight…
You have to be carefully taught."

My great grandmother Mazal had encountered discrimination for her Yemenite culture and looks when she first came to Israel in 1882. I certainly didn't want to perpetuate it through ignorance and distrust of these beautiful newly-found Jews, the Beta Israel, just because their skin was black.

Chapter 12

FAMILY CONFERENCES SEEMED TO happen quite
often in our close-knit clan. Although Israel is a tiny country, when you look at it on the map and in reality, there
are great distances to be travelled when your families are
far-flung, as our family is. It is still our custom to get everyone involved in a difficult situation. Dikla was 20 and
needed no one's permission to get married, but she felt
she could not do so without her parents' blessing, which
they were not willing to give. So a meeting of the clan
was arranged, this time at Dina and Yitzhak's home in the
development town of Rosh haAyin, where Dikla and
Menelik had met and worked together. There was good
bus service to Petah Tikvah, and Rosh haAyin was close
by.

We understood some of our cousins' concerns.
Menelik admitted that part of his distant family had been
forced to convert to Christianity. A German Jew named
Henry Aaron Stern, who had himself converted, came to
Ethiopia in 1860 to "save" the Falashas. He was a mis-
sionary and had promised Emperor Theodore of Ethiopia
that he would bring them into the Coptic Church. However, he fell foul of the Emperor and was punished, but
there were continuous pressures from other missionaries
to convert, and from poverty and hunger some had suc-

cumbed in an effort to improve their miserable circumstances.

However Menelik assured us that his close, immediate family had remained steadfastly Jewish. His forebears
had adopted the native language of Ge'ez or old Ethopic
for sacred writings and had spoken at first in the old
Cushite languages. Later Jews used the national language
of Amharic, but they still clung to their Jewish traditions.

Dikla and Menelik were not present, at her parents'
request, nor were her younger siblings. Dina sat at the
table, nervously pleating and fraying a paper napkin, not
touching the food she had set out for the visitors. Yitzhak
sat grim-faced, his jaws clenched tight.

"What are we to do?" Dina asked tearfully. "She
won't listen to us. She's determined to marry him, and
he's so unsuitable."

"Why?" I couldn't help asking. "Just because he's
black?"

"I would be so embarrassed. I can't deal with it!"

Kobi, although only family through his marriage to
me, nevertheless felt compelled to comment. "I found
him a very likeable young man," he offered. "He is re-
spectful, educated, hard-working, religious. Don't those
qualities count?"

Yitzhak spoke for the first time. "If it were your daughter, you'd feel differently," he said bitterly. "Dikla is our
firstborn. She was such a bright, happy little girl. We had
such plans for her…"

"But we don't own our children," another cousin
added. "What do they say: 'We make plans and G-d
laughs!'"

"I wish it could have been Doron," Dina whispered,
casting a resentful look at his parents.

His mother looked sad. "That would have been nice.
But Doron met this girl Liat in the Army and they are

inseparable. She's not Yemenite either," she added defensively.

"But she's white!"

"Well, yes. But we would have preferred a Yemenite daughter-in-law too."

"There's no comparison," Yitzhak replied. "What will their children be ... half-casts."

I was shocked. "Yitzhak, that's a horrible thing to say. Their children will probably be beautiful, and unquestionably Jewish. Everyone will accept them. And when the time comes, you'll love them too. I understand it's a shock. I found it difficult too at first," I admitted, remembering my own embarrassment at our first meeting. "But once you talk to him and see what a good person he is, and how they love each other, and realize all the things they have in common in their work and so on, his Ethiopian background no longer matters."

The family gave opinions back and forth for nearly an hour, some supporting Yitzhak and Dina, others more tolerant and understanding. Finally great-aunt Ruchama banged on the table. All eyes turned to her, still a dignified and commanding presence despite her years.

"I was the second one in the family to break the Yemenite chain," she offered. "First there was mother's sister Miriam, who married a farmer from Poland. When my grandfather Djeddi arrived in Palestine and learned of it, he said he would never forgive her. He did, of course, once he got used to the idea. Then, when my mother told him that I wanted to marry Menachem Bak, an Ashkenazi, I thought he would have a stroke. He absolutely forbid it even to be discussed. But I'll tell you this. Even at the risk of alienation from my whole family, whom I loved dearly, I did not waver. I married the man I loved and we were together for forty years until he passed away, and even Djeddi learned to admire him and often consulted him on all kinds of business matters, even *Halacha*. You have a choice. Either you welcome him into the family and keep your daughter's love; or you maintain this stiff-necked attitude that will split your family, cause untold bitterness, and deny you your future grandchildren."

Somebody clapped. Soon everyone was talking at once. Yitzhak slowly nodded his head. Dina was crying, but smiling at the same time. The matter was resolved. Another family crisis had been averted!

Chapter 13

MUCH PLANNING went into Dikla's wedding and we were all involved. There was no question that she would definitely have a henna ceremony. She knew her family would be inconsolable if she denied them this Yemenite tradition, and Menelik was anxious to please them. He explained that even in Ethiopia, the bride's fingernails are dyed with henna, which is called "esosela" in Amharic. It is used both for beauty and as a charm for protection against evil. I had to smile when he said to me: "You know, Dikla and I are quite old to be getting married. Quite a lot of young people back home are betrothed when the girl is 13 or 14, and the boy 16 or 17. They usually wait a year or two to marry though." I told him that my great grandmother Mazal was married at 14 in Yemen too, and her marriage was very happy despite the difficult journey to Jerusalem and the early hardships in making a living. But by today's standards, he and Dikla did seem young to be getting married, even though she was 20 and he was 24. Perhaps today we get caught up in too many responsibilities, like finding affordable housing, Army service, careers, livelihoods etc. that dampen the ardor. Often marriage has to wait on these practical considerations.

However, now that Yitzhak and Dina had given their blessing, the whole extended family wanted to help with the arrangements, including Menelik's married brother and sister and their families in Ashkelon. It would have been wonderful if his parents could have joined us, but they still remained in their village near Lake Tana, awaiting permission to come to Israel.

We tried to learn from him about the "sarg," their wedding ceremony, and agreed that a "qes," the Beta Israel's Rabbi and teacher, would participate in the ceremony alongside an Israeli Rabbi. We couldn't, however, accommodate all their customs, such as seven days of wedding festivities. They would have to be satisfied with our custom of "sheva brachot," the seven blessings. However, Menelik decided to include the "keshera" or tying ceremony, in which the "qes" publicly arranges two cords that are the length of the groom's body, and then ties them around his forehead. One cord is white for chastity, and one red to signify the bride's virginity.

Dikla looked truly beautiful on her wedding day, as all brides do, radiant with happiness. The henna ceremony had taken place a week earlier, when she was dressed in a caftan of gold and silver thread with embroidered leggings. She wore the Yemenite "gargush," a headdress adorned with gold, silver, and pearls and with fresh flowers framing the tall cone. And of course, outshining her other jewelry, the gold pomegranate pendant I had pledged Mazal to pass on to all the brides in our family at their henna ceremony.

I could still remember her words: "I am giving you a sacred trust. Every bride in the ben-Yechiya family should wear it at her henna ceremony. I know that many of them will not marry Yemenites, but perhaps out of respect for my memory, they will maintain the tradition. It is a very lovely one ... the dab of henna representing a seal on the hand and the heart." She had explained to me, only 18 years old at the time, that the pomegranate, with its many seeds, symbolized fertility. My great grandfather Ezra, whom I had never known, had fashioned the necklace with its delicate gold filigree pomegranate, as a wedding gift for Mazal. She must have had a premonition that she would not live to see other brides in the family. I remember she held my hand as she said, "I would like to think that you will pass it on and that my pomegranate pendant will be a talisman for good for all the generations yet to come." That was the last conversation I had with her. She died, in the fullness of years, soon after my wedding.

Today, Dikla was dressed very differently than at her henna ceremony. The caftan and headdress had been replaced by a lustrous white satin gown, modest but opulent, and a long white veil fastened to her hair with white magnolias. All the jewelry had been removed except for the pomegranate pendant, which brought tears to my eyes and to those of many of our kinsfolk who remembered Mazal and the sense of tradition that she had instilled in us all. Led by an Israeli Rabbi, with the "qes" at his side, the ceremony was the modern Orthodox one, even to the breaking of the wine glass which was not part of either the Yemenite nor the Beta Israel tradition. I looked to see if Dikla's parents were still unhappy about the union, but despite their tear-filled eyes, they were smiling under the "chupah." First the Rabbi read the "ketubah," then the "qes" blessed the wine, and then Yemenite friends of Yitzhak's family and Beta Israel friends of Menelik's alternated in reading the benedictions. Everyone sang "Should I forget thee, O Jerusalem, let my right hand forget its cunning." There were happy tears, emotional hugs and kisses, as the bride and groom walked back up the aisle, to partake privately of their first meal together as man and wife.

In my mind, I conjured up the face of Mazal, and imagined her smiling down from heaven, blessing Dikla, her beautiful descendant. Then I looked around at the guests, some olive-skinned Yemenites like us; some black Ethiopians; some blonde Ashkenazim … and in my heart I gave thanks. We were all Jews. We had all arrived to live in Eretz Israel. Some of us had undergone unimaginable hardships in our journey and our absorption. But we had all come home. We had survived. "Blessed art Thou, O Lord our G-d, King of the Universe, who has kept us alive, sustained us and enabled us to come to this season."

Missing Jerusalem

It was not for long
I left you,
But each parting
Is a small death.

Now I am returning
To leafy arms of pine,
A kiss of sunshine -
Gold on grey stone.

The sighing wind
Whispers secrets to me;
Jerusalem's perfume
Is my embrace.

I have missed you...
Missed your gentle blessing,
But now I am returning -
Coming home!

Chapter 14

IT WAS 1973 AND my family was growing up. Shira Mazal was 16, on the way to becoming a beautiful young lady. Uri was 14 and Moshe was already learning for his bar-mitzvah, which would take place in the coming year. We had reopened "The Pomegranate Pendant" in Jerusalem's Old City, and Kobi was enjoying its success. Re-creating Mazal's dream had been his idea, but many members of the family were staffing it and supplying its stock of arts and crafts and jewelry. I was sure my great grandparents, Mazal and Ezra, would have been thrilled to see so many of their descendants making a living from the store; and all the tourists as well as locals who entered its doors to buy Jewish and Israeli gifts for friends and loved ones or unique artifacts to adorn their own homes.

My husband ran the bookstore section, and I was the buyer of Judaica items that our relatives could not produce themselves. It was not a demanding job and it gave me plenty of time to run my home, tend my herb garden and spend time with my children.

Shira Mazal seemed to turn to me a lot for advice as she grew older. Blossoming womanhood seemed to bond us closer which I found gratifying as she'd always been such an independent child. One day she sat and watched me as I weeded the garden, meditating on whatever occupies the mind of 16-year-olds. "What should I do when I leave school?" she suddenly asked me. "I've only got two more years."

"You should do whatever interests you the most."

"Should I do "sherut leumi" first?" (This is the national service option for religious girls in Israel, enabling them to do one or two years of community service instead of serving in the Army.)

"What a question! Of course you'll do 'sherut leumi.' In fact I hope you'll do two years," I answered somewhat sharply. "You can't just take from your country and society without giving something back. I feel very strongly that it is incumbent on all of us to help our country in some voluntary way. You can't be like the girls who evade it altogether."

"And after that?"

"Well, you might get married like Dikla did, or you might go to University. The two things are not mutually exclusive," I pointed out.

"I think I'd like to be a doctor," she said after a pause. "Maybe a pediatrician. But I don't think I could do it."

"Why not?"

"Oh, you know. So many years of study. Who can commit themselves to one thing for seven years or more."

"Many have," I replied. "Some people, like Theodor Herzl, devoted their whole lives to a dream. He said, 'If you will it, it shall not remain a dream.' I really believe that."

"Do you?" she was thoughtful. "He burned himself out though. He was only 44 when he died," she reminded me.

I laid down my trowel and weeding fork. I felt a talk on Zionism was more important because not a day went by without my feeling an enormous sense of privilege in living in the re-born State of Israel, especially in Jerusalem and even more especially in the Old City which we had regained from the Jordanians only six years earlier.

"There is a big difference between just filling in time in this life with making money and enjoying yourself as opposed to doing something fulfilling and selfless. Herzl was a man from a secular background who really stumbled into his role of greatness almost by accident. He was a journalist in Vienna when he was sent by his newspaper to Paris in 1894 to cover the trial of Dreyfus, an innocent and outstanding Army officer framed and accused of treason simply because he was a Jew. For the first time Herzl became aware of the rampant anti-Semitism in Europe, and he had a vision to create a Jewish homeland where his people would find a safe haven. From that moment on, he devoted his whole life to making it happen."

"What exactly did he do?"

"Herzl convened the first Zionist Congress in 1897. He went from country to country, negotiating with the Turkish Sultan in Constantinople, the Lord Chamberlain in London, the German Kaiser ... some of them took bribes and all made him promises that they had no intention of keeping. A lesser man would have given up, but the on-going outbreaks of violence and the terrible Kishniev pogrom in 1903 only fueled his determination to keep going. When he felt he would never regain Eretz Israel, he was even willing to settle for a homeland in Uganda if Jews would be safe there from persecution."

"But he never lived to see his dream come true."

"That's true," I admitted. "Luckily he didn't live to see the horror of the Holocaust either. That would have completely destroyed him. But it was because of his vision that others took up his dream. If he were alive today, he would see a wonderful land with our kibbutzim leading the world in agriculture. He would see villages and cities with buildings like skyscrapers; thriving industry; high-tech; science and art and literature... A tiny country, but with what magnificent achievements. He left the Jewish people a legacy that challenged them not to let his dream die. It all started with the vision of just one man.

"If you will it, it shall not remain a dream," Shira Mazal echoed thoughtfully. "So where shall I begin?"

"Doing your homework might be a good start," I laughed, as I gathered up my gardening tools and went inside to prepare dinner.

From My Balcony

This is where I keep a dawn vigil.

Thru' a tracery of pines
Jerusalem is awash in pearly dawn.

Geraniums are sentinels, guarding
My wrought iron railing,
While flamboyant crimson flowers
Shed petals on the stone.

I am part of the scene,
Yet hover high above it
As the city wakes to a new day.

I hear the echoes of its history,
Smell the fragrance of its hills,
Taste the mist and soft-falling dew -
Both participant and witness.

My balcony is peaceful
In these early hours.
Only a dog stirs, in the street below,
breaking the silence.

For a short time yet
Jerusalem is mine...
And I cherish the ownership
Of this shining, precious jewel.

Chapter 15

THE YEAR WAS NOT going well, not for the family and not for Israel. It began with the death of my great-aunt Ruchama. Since Mazal's death, she had taken on the role of family matriarch. Unlike her mother, she had started out in life as an introverted, sensitive girl. Her loves, apart from her husband Menachem and her four children, had been nature and painting. Although she was close to her brothers and their families, by inclination she was a loner. It was only a sense of responsibility that in latter years had given her this role. The family turned to her for advice and she tried to counsel them in the way she thought Mazal would have done had she still been alive. That was why she had intercepted in the rift between Dikla and her parents, urging them to accept Menelik as their son-in-law. Family unity was important to her, and she had a quiet wisdom we all respected.

So it was not only her children and grandchildren who mourned her. We all felt it to a greater or lesser degree. Each time I worked in my herb garden, I remembered it was Ruchama who had helped to get me started. I suppose everyone is remembered for something they did in life. I hoped that when my time came, I would leave the kind of legacy that she did ... a strong feeling for family; a helping hand whenever it was needed; wise counsel and the sense of wonder that she never lost. It enabled her, even in old age, to acknowledge the beauty all around us, in the trembling of a leaf; a dewdrop in the heart of a rose; the perfume of jasmine on the night air; the heart-catching beauty of a purple bouganvillea in full bloom ....

Ruchama passed away in the Hebrew month of Sivan or May in 1972. It was a few days after the terrorist attack at Lod airport, and I wondered if the shock had hastened her death as one of the victims had been her neighbor. Twelve people were dead and fifty wounded, most of them seriously, when a Japanese gang fired a sub-machine gun and lobbed hand grenades into the crowded Arrivals Hall. They had arrived in Israel on an Air France plane from Paris and Rome at 10:30 p.m. At the baggage carousel, they suddenly produced Kalatchnikov rifles from their suitcases and burst through the hall, while also lobbing hand grenades. Passengers scrambled for cover while the terrorists ran towards the glass wall in the building where crowds were waiting for the arriving passengers. Then they ran onto the airfield, throwing grenades at a Scanair plane. One terrorist was captured, one killed himself, and one seemed to have escaped. The Marxist Popular Front for the Liberation of Palestine (PFLP) claimed that its "guerillas" were responsible.

It was a horrifying incident that shook the whole of Israel to its core. The captured Japanese was named Kozo Okamoto, and he was sentenced to life imprisonment in Ramle Prison.

But there was an even worse tragedy, if that is possible, a few months later, when nine Israeli athletes competing in the Olympic Games in Munich were killed by eight Arab gunmen, as were the four terrorists and one West German policeman, plus another two Israeli members of the delegation who were murdered by the terrorists in the Olympic Village. Initially the Israeli athletes were taken as hostages, intending to fly them to an Arab country, probably Libya. The deaths occurred in a bungled attempt by the German police to rescue them and kill the terrorists. Amazingly, and very callously, the Games resumed after just a 24-hour suspension. It seemed to us that in the eyes of the world, Israeli lives were very cheap.

As 1972 drew to a close, the mood in Israel was very somber. None of us could have foretold, however, just how much worse the next year would prove to be.

Chapter 16

THE YEAR BEGAN ON a happy note, with our youngest son Moshe's bar-mitzvah. It was hard to believe that our baby had grown up so quickly and, at least in the eyes of our Jewish faith, was soon to be regarded as a man. His father would no longer have to be responsible for his actions, at least in theory. He had always been a mischievous little boy, and I suppose we'd indulged him a lot simply because he was our youngest.

The portion of the Bible that he would read in the synagogue was called "Tzav," the Hebrew word for "command." With Hebrew being our native tongue, it didn't pose the problem it did for boys overseas, but he still had to learn to chant it according to the special musical notes called "ta'amim" or "trop." His father was his teacher, and Kobi's melodious voice, with its Yemenite origins and inflections, had been passed on to both our sons. We had a "kiddush" after the service with wine and cakes for all the congregation and a party for family and Moshe's friends the next day. Although he pretended it wasn't important to him, his eyes shone when he saw all the gifts. Some were computer games, his very favorite. Not many were books as everyone knew we owned a book shop. Some of them were very modest, but he was just as excited with them as he tore off the pretty paper and colored ribbons.

I insisted that he make a list of who had given him what, so that he could later write "thank you" notes to everyone. "Nobody does that anymore," he informed me. "That may be true, but it's good manners. Surely if some-one goes to the trouble of bringing you a gift, they should have their generosity and kindness acknowledged." He nodded reluctantly. "Well maybe we could just buy a bunch of "thank you" cards and I'll sign them?"

When I shook my head, he knew better than to insist. Bringing up children with the values I believed in was hard work, but was probably the most important work I was called on to do.

After all the excitement of the bar-mitzvah was over, we were able to notice what was happening outside our family circle. There were rumors of the possibility of an attack on Israel by Syria and Egypt, but our Intelligence service assessed it as being unlikely. This was despite the fact that a month earlier, their armies had bolstered their forces alarmingly. Nevertheless a decision was taken to beef up our forces on the Golan Heights and to put the Army on alert. Despite this, Prime Minister Golda Meir had planned on a trip to Australia the day after Rosh Hashana, our New Year, seemingly oblivious to the dan-ger we were facing, and she went ahead with it. As we approached Yom Kippur, the Day of Atonement, ten days later, we learned that huge Egyptian and Syrian forces, including armored columns, were moving to the border. Still the Intelligence insisted that an attack was "low prob-ability."

Three days before Yom Kippur, our charismatic De-fence Minister, Moshe Dayan, did a tour of the Golan Heights and warned Syria that we would retaliate harshly if they attacked us. The Chief of Staff, David Elazar, wanted to call up the Reserves, but the Government did not agree. Like all Israeli wives and mothers, I was glad and only too willing to believe that the enemy was either "posturing" or carrying out meaningless maneuvers.

The Government only began to take the situation seriously two days before Yom Kippur when Israel received a dramatic report from a reliable source close to the Egyptian leadership who said that we were about to be attacked by both Egypt and Syria. So there was a partial call-up of the Reserves, but Kobi hadn't received his papers.

I could not conceive that we would have to face yet another war. We were such a peace-loving nation that was not permitted to live in peace. When we greeted each other, it was with the word "shalom" meaning "peace," and every week we wished each other "Shabbat Shalom" … a Sabbath of peace. Still we could not believe that war was again imminent, not even two days before Yom Kippur. At the most, we were informed by our leadership, there might be a few skirmishes on the border areas.

Yom Kippur began as a calm, quiet day. Moshe was fasting fully for the first time and very proud of himself. Kobi took the two boys to synagogue with him at 7 a.m. Shira Mazal and I went a little later. There was a break of two hours in the prayers at noon, so we went home to rest. At 2 p.m. we were all back in synagogue.

What happened next was unbelievable. We heard a disturbance and looked down at the men's section. Soldiers had rushed in and men, still wearing their prayer shawls, hurried out with them to the waiting jeeps we could see through the window. I grabbed my daughter's hand as I saw Kobi rush out with them. Jeeps … driving on the holiest day of the year! Not even secular Jews publicly desecrated Yom Kippur by driving, and here were our Orthodox, most pious men, getting into jeeps. I had heard the expression, "my heart was in my throat" and now I understood its literal meaning. I felt I was either going to throw up or faint as I saw Kobi and many others leave without even a backward glance. Shortly afterwards, we understood, as the air raid siren wailed and we had to go to the nearest air raid shelter, many of us crying and all of us terrified.

Only the next day did we know any details. Egypt and Syria had launched a massive attack. We were told that 200 Egyptian war planes had attacked our IDF forces in Sinai. At the same time, their ground forces crossed the Suez Canal with rubber boats, and they constructed bridges to bring over even more forces, all equipped with anti-tank rockets. They had 100,000 soldiers and dozens of tanks. We had just 8,000 men, mostly older ones from the Reserves, like Kobi, no longer fighting-fit. Most of the tanks we had deployed near the Canal were ambushed by Egypt and destroyed. The Egyptians captured most of our IDF outposts.

The attack on the Syrian front was another terrifying surprise. Their planes attacked our units on the Golan Heights and artillery shelled our settlements. Syrian tanks captured the Golan with almost no resistance. Wave after wave of our planes attacked the advancing Syrian army, but missiles downed the planes. Syrian commandos in helicopters conquered our outpost on top of Mount Hermon. This was a most terrible loss as it had always been known as "the eyes of Israel." Many of our Intelligence soldiers were taken prisoner and their advanced electronic equipment was sent to Damascus.

The situation was grim. Would this be the war we would lose? Had G-d deserted us on the very day the House of Israel was praying for mercy and forgiveness for our sins, communally and individually? It was only knowing that I needed to be strong for our children that prevented me from complete collapse. We hadn't heard from Kobi and we knew that our losses had to be tremendous. What was happening to our people? Would this be the time that our enemies managed, as they so often threatened, to throw us all into the sea?

Chapter 17

THIS WAS NOT A QUICK, decisive and miraculous war like we had fought in '67, defeating our enemies in just six days. It began on October 6th, 1973. Probably October 7th, when we began the counter-offensive, was the most difficult day. Our small IDF units on the southern front faced five Egyptian armored and infantry divisions of 400 tanks and 100,000 soldiers. Our IDF reserves began arriving at the front, and the regular forces fought with whatever they had left to prevent the entire sector from falling.

In the north it was even worse with two Syrian tank columns moving deep into the Golan Heights. They were only seven kilometers from Lake Kinneret. Our entire air force was sent to ward off the Syrian assault.

Although Chief of Staff David Elazar said, "We will go on fighting until we break their bones," our losses were very heavy and our morale very low. Four hundred of our tanks were destroyed, and we were not told how many men had fallen or were wounded, but we knew it had to be in the hundreds. Moshe Dayan wanted to inform the public of how grave our situation was, but Prime Minister Golda Meir would not allow it. Nor would she accept his resignation when he wanted to tender it.

We had no idea where Kobi was, and the atmosphere

at home was very tense. Shira Mazal reacted to her father's absence by becoming withdrawn and sullen. Moshe had temper tantrums which were quite contrary to his usual sunny nature. But it was Uri who was giving me the most trouble.

"I'm nearly 15. I'm big for my age. I could pass for 18. I need to enlist," he informed me almost every morning when I tried to get him ready for school.

"You might think you look 18, but you're not even 15 yet."

"You could vouch for me," he insisted. "Tell them I'm 18, that there's a mistake on my birth certificate."

"And what would that accomplish?"

"I could go and be with Abba. Maybe help him. Maybe protect him."

"Wouldn't it be the other way around? That as well as fighting and trying to remain unharmed himself, he'd also have to worry about you?" I asked gently. "And who would help me at home, with both my men gone?" Even though it was a nonsensical scenario, I didn't want to insult his manhood, or laugh at him. Already there were tears in his eyes. I understood how impotent he felt, because in comparison with putting your life on the line defending your country, my role of looking after the family and working in the store paled into insignificance.

Uri was not content to let the matter rest. "Back in '47 and '48, when we fought the War of Independence, boys and girls younger than me were working for Hagana, even for Lehi and Etzel!"

I couldn't contradict him. I remembered my great-uncle Shalom and his son Mattanyah, my Uncle Matti. At the age of 16 he had left school, just as his father had. His parents labelled him "uncontrollable" because he had a secret life that he refused to share with them, disappearing sometimes in the middle of the night and often not coming home for days at a time. Mazal had taken him to live with her and promised to protect his privacy, albeit with many misgivings about his activities. When he finally admitted to her what he was doing, she was faint with fear. She had suspected that he might be involved with the Hagana, but he was with Etzel, the most extreme element fighting the British. Etzel, which was the abbreviation for Irgun Tzva'i Leumi, was the militant resistance movement whose motto was "Fight Terror with Terror". Although the family thought of him as just a kid, as I did with Uri, he felt that he was a soldier in the eyes of David Raziel, the Etzel Commander-in-Chief. Matti survived the fighting, but his best friend Yitzhak did not. Yitzhak was the grandson of Sarah Bak, who had been Mazal's closest friend and mentor, a boy who had seen his father, brother, and baby niece all murdered in Hebron.

Etzel activists, many of them as Uri had stated, youths of tender teenage years, had blown up railway lines and telephone exchanges; had taken down British flags and replaced them with the Star of David; had taken part in reprisal attacks on Arabs ... their activities were dangerous beyond belief, but their ideal of a safe homeland for the Jewish people drove them beyond the limits of safety.

I knew that Uri had heard some of these stories, even from Matti himself, so it would have been foolish to deny them. "My dear," I told him gently, "your time will come. Sadly, with enemies on every border, Israel will always need an army. In three years, you'll be in uniform, without any need to lie about your age. Until then, try to concentrate on your studies so that when peace comes, you can have a good profession and livelihood and lead a normal life. You need to have some fun at your age." He shook his head pessimistically, and even to me the words did not ring true.

In other countries, boys and girls his age were going to parties, enjoying their teenage years in a myriad of ways.

Only in Israel were they never given that chance. Even when not officially at war as we were now, we never had peace from terrorist attacks on our borders and within them. At 18, our youth all knew that years of Army service were required of them, and that they might not live to enjoy the fruits of peace if it ever came.

He left for school with shoulders slumped, while I felt the weight of his sadness and impotence long after he had gone. There was no news of Kobi, and there was nothing in the daily news bulletins to lighten our fears. We were a nation that stood alone.

Chapter 18

THE DAYS PASSED SLOWLY at that bitter time in our history. The Egyptians were showing remarkable staying power. On October 11th, the sixth day of the war, the IDF was ordered to launch a big assault on Syria. We were bombing targets around Damascus including their airports, military bases, and oil refineries. At the same time we had a major victory in that the IDF had conquered the Golan Heights. The Syrians finally retreated, leaving behind 900 tanks.

Perhaps the tide was finally turning. We regained the territories we had lost before the war, and even some more land inside Syria. America had come to our aid, and we were grateful for her help in our struggle to withstand the aggression. In contrast, the British and French arms embargo was cynical and harmful, while the Soviets continued to airlift weapons to Syria and Egypt. The aim of the Arab States, as it had been in 1967, was to destroy, totally, the State of Israel.

Unless you have personally experienced it, you cannot imagine the toll that war takes on a family. Although we hadn't heard from Kobi directly, we would sometimes get phone calls or visits from soldiers who had been fighting with him and had a few days leave. The IDF is an army of brothers, and it was a priority with them to send messages of comfort to comrades' families whenever they had the opportunity, and to take back with them letters and small care passages of chocolate, candies, cookies … anything we could think of that might sweeten our loved ones' lives in the bitter environment they were inhabiting. They were not allowed to tell us where he was, or any other vital information that might be of aid to the enemy, but in those stressful days, we clutched at whatever straws we could.

Every day Moshe asked me, "Is Abba coming home today?" and his eyes would fill with tears when I was forced sadly to shake my head. "Well, when?" he would demand repeatedly, and when I couldn't give him an answer, he would vent his frustration by kicking at the leg of a chair or a toy that was lying on the floor. I tried to cuddle him and reassure him, but he'd push me away angrily and I'd feel my own eyes fill with tears, both at his rejection and my own feelings of helplessness, insecurity and sadness.

Many nights I would dream that I'd been widowed. I'd even envisage myself at a grave in the Military cemetery… and I'd wake up in the morning with an inexplicable weight of terror and sorrow and loneliness. It would take me a few minutes to realize it had only been a dream, but I was still terrified it might be a premonition of what was to come.

As in the War of Independence in 1948, we were glued to our radios and the latest news was the only topic of conversation. After we had launched an assault on Syria, the tide seemed to be turning, and then on October 18th, paratroopers crossed the Suez Canal in rubber boats at the gap between the Second and Third Egyptian armies, followed by tanks that crossed the Canal on rafts. Sharon's brigade moved north towards Ismailiya. We could have had a decisive victory, but on October 22nd, the UN Security Council imposed a cease-fire after Israel had surrounded the entire Third Army.

The most difficult battle was at a site called the "Chinese Farm". Our paratrooper unit, under Lieutenant Colonel Yitzchak Mordechai, entered a death trap by falling into an ambush by an Egyptian division. Our losses were tremendous. Each time the losses were broadcast, without names, I was paranoid with fear. We had only heard from Kobi once, a frustrating phone call, with the crackle of static making it impossible to understand most of what he was saying. Meant to reassure us, all it accomplished was to deepen my anxiety.

Finally, on November 11th, a cease-fire agreement was signed at Kilometer 101, on the Suez-Cairo road. There were no celebrations because we had lost 2,600 soldiers and 7,000 were wounded, some so badly that their lives, as well as their limbs, were shattered. Egypt had taken 233 Israeli POWs, while we had 8,300 of their prisoners. They were exchanged on November 15th.

Kobi came home, this time limping from shrapnel in his right leg. Just as he'd been after the Six-Day War five years earlier, he was very quiet and introverted. He spent the first weeks visiting families of comrades who had fallen, and each time he came home, we would sense that he needed to be alone with his thoughts. At dinner one night, Uri reached across the table and touched his hand. "Abba," he said, his voice thick with emotion, "I wish I could have been there alongside you during the fighting."

Kobi's eyes filled with tears. "I hope you never have to fight, my son. Maybe this time we'll have a lasting peace. Maybe the Arabs will finally leave us alone, just to live ordinary lives like other people."

We could hope, but we didn't really believe it. I thought of Golda Meir's words: "We will only have peace when the Arabs love their children more than they hate us."

Chapter 19

SLOWLY, IN THE AFTERMATH of the war, our lives quietened down and we returned to some kind of routine and normalcy. There was even excitement when film star Danny Kaye arrived here, with French singer Enrico Macias, to perform for our troops and the wounded in hospitals.

Eventually Kobi also returned to work at "The Pomegranate Pendant". With peace, the store was doing well as tourists were flocking into Jerusalem's Old City. Kobi had closed our other bookstore, and transferred his stock, so that the shelves were laden not only with religious tomes, but also books on Jewish history and Israel's wars, alongside kosher cookery books and even brightly illustrated children's books that made the Jewish festivals come alive for them.

We had a showcase full of beautiful jewelry, much of which had been made by Orpah, my aunt Miriam's daughter. To be true to our heritage, most of it was in the Yemenite tradition, with delicate pomegranates in silver and gold as necklaces or exquisite earrings. There were also amber necklaces and filigree hands to ward off the "Evil Eye", and bracelets made from silver beads. But there were also more modern designs that she had learned at Bezalel and these were equally popular.

Our stock kept growing as various other family members contributed embroidered challah cloths and matzah covers; velvet bags to hold a "tallit" (prayer shawl) and "tefillin" (phylacteries); unusual mezuzah cases and all kinds of gift cards for special occasions, created and hand-painted by great-Aunt Ruchama's granddaughter Einav, who had inherited her artistic talents.

A family business is something very special, particularly as so many of the extended family were involved in it, even peripherally. Many of them would have known economic hardship if we hadn't found a way to use whatever strengths they had. They weren't all craftsmen, but some distant cousins worked part-time on commission for us as buyers, to supplement their income. They would travel to outlying Yemenite communities and sometimes bring us leather items, occasional woven pieces and often exquisite embroidery. These were things not found in the usual retail shops, and Israelis, as well as tourists, were buying them to give as gifts on special occasions. Everyone who worked for us in any capacity was family, either through birth or marriage. It was not charity, for they pulled their weight, and I was sure that Mazal and Ezra, our wonderful forebears who had started the enterprise, were giving us blessings from heaven that helped our success.

Since Menelik had joined our family, the store also carried the work of two of his cousins from Ashkelon who were Ethiopian sculptors. We had figurines in pottery and wood of their people, engaged in village life back home, and miniatures of King Solomon and the Queen of Sheba, and these elicited a lot of interest. We also had drawings and paintings of Ethiopian villages and hunting scenes that were very popular, as well as some woven baskets. Everything we displayed was handmade by artisans and craftsmen, nothing was mass-produced in factories. Our gifts were unique, but sometimes expensive, as they often represented many hours of intricate, painstaking labor.

Of course the store was closed on the Jewish holidays and on Shabbat, but our customers may have been puzzled to find it closed also one Thursday. The reason was a happy one ... Dikla had given birth to a baby boy, and we all wanted to attend the "brit milah" (circumcision) ceremony in Rosh haAyin.

All Dinah and Yitzhak's original apprehensions had long been buried, and they had become very fond of their Ethiopian son-in-law, Menelik. Now, a grandson was to bring them great joy and they had arranged a celebration in a hall next to the synagogue, large enough to hold all their extended family, as well as their friends and friends of their children.

The baby was gorgeous, not quite black, but with skin the color of rich, dark chocolate and a head of curly black hair. Now eight days old, he was to be admitted into the covenant of Abraham. The ritual of circumcision is commanded in the Bible:

> "G-d further said to Abraham ... Such shall be the covenant between Me and your offspring to follow which you shall keep... throughout the generations, every male among you shall be circumcised at the age of eight days." (Gen.17:9-12)

The "brit milah" is a joyous occasion, but Dikla, like all new mothers, was nervous and a bit tearful. The baby was brought into the synagogue and, in the traditional way, handed to the "mohel" who would perform the ritual.

Everyone greeted the infant with the Biblical verse: "Blessed be he who cometh in the name of the Lord", from Psalm 118. Yitzhak was given the honor of being the "sandek," the one who holds the baby in his lap during the ceremony. He sat in the "sandek's" special chair, which was next to the chair for the Prophet Elijah, who, according to our tradition, attends every circumcision and protects the infants from danger.

In this case, the "mohel" was a Yemenite friend of Yitzhak's. He recited some appropriate verses and made the benediction: "Praised art Thou, O Lord our G-d, King of the Universe, who sanctified us by His commandments, and commanded us to perform the rite of circumcision." Then, after the ritual, Menelik repeated the words from the Talmud: "Praised art Thou, O Lord our G-d, King of the Universe, who has sanctified us by His commandments and commanded us to make him enter into the covenant of Abraham our father." We all responded: "Even as he has entered the covenant, so may he enter the study of the Torah, the marriage canopy and the performance of good deeds."

The baby, by this time, was letting out a mighty wail, and was given some wine to suck, on a piece of cotton, which he seemed to enjoy, as everyone waited quietly to hear his name. "...Let his name be called in Israel, "Israel the son of Menelik. Let his father rejoice in him that came forth from his loins, and the mother be glad with the fruit of her womb."

As Dikla whisked the baby away to an adjoining room to nurse and cuddle him, there was a lot of hand-shaking, kisses and cries of "Mazal tov" as we all streamed into the hall for the festivities. Long tables were set with all kinds of delicacies. It was heart-warming to see Yitzhak and Dina beaming with pride and happiness, greeting all the guests from both sides of the family.

When everyone had eaten and drunk their fill, Menelik rose to speak. "This is a wonderful day for me, next to my wedding day, the happiest day in my life. Only one more thing would make it perfect: if my dear father and mother, my brother and two sisters who are still in Ethiopia, could also have been here today. I pray that they will be able to come soon. They probably would have been puzzled by today's 'brit milah' for things are done differently in Ethiopia. When Dikla was ready to give birth, she would have entered a special birthing hut, which was called 'yaras gojo'. Two midwives would have assisted her, and when the baby was born, they would have emitted twelve shouts of joy for a boy, and only nine if it had been a girl. The whole village would have been waiting to hear the news. Then Dikla would have moved to another hut for 32 more days, just as it's written in Leviticus 12: 2-5. Only on the 40th day would our baby have been named, with blessings from the 'Arde'et', the Falasha Book of the Disciples.

"We gave our son just one name, 'Israel'. For all of us, Eretz Israel has been the focus of our longing from time immemorial. I, and some of my family, have been privileged to come here, just as Dikla's family did from Yemen. We feel it is indeed a great privilege and a blessing, and it is here that I have received the greatest gifts I could imagine, my beautiful wife Dikla and my son, Israel ben Menelik."

There were many wet eyes when he sat down, including mine, as Dina and Yitzhak stood up and kissed their son-in-law.

I noticed Doron and his new wife among the guests, and thought it had all turned out for the best. Dikla had believed Doron was her "beshert," her soul mate, but as they say, we make plans and G-d laughs. The Jewish people are like a mosaic made up of small stones. Sometimes we try to fit in pieces that are not meant to be connected, but eventually we are shown the perfect complement. A "brit milah" is an emotional experience. We see a new soul joining our people, welcomed with love and blessings.

There was now music and dancing, and I went over and joined the women's circle, letting the happiness wash over me to the beat and rhythm of the vibrant music.

Part
Two

Seeds
Of The
Pomegranate

Chapter 20

WE APPROACHED ROSH HASHANA 5738 ... September 1978 ...with some apprehension. The year had begun badly for Israel.. In March, a Fatah squad in boats reached the shore of Ma'agan Michael killing an American tourist, a talented nature photographer. Then they divided into two units. They first stopped a taxi on the Coastal Highway, murdered the driver and set off on a trip of murder. The second unit stopped a bus, killing some of the passengers and taking the rest hostage. On the drive to Tel Aviv, the terrorists threw hand grenades and fired at passing cars. When the police forced the bus to halt at a road block, they opened fire on the policemen. Our anti-terror squad stormed the bus, killing the terrorists, but the bus caught fire and the passengers were burned alive. There were 35 people killed and dozens wounded.

Only three months later, on June 2nd, a bomb exploded on a bus to Jerusalem, killing another six people and wounding 19. It seemed our history would always be written in blood.

Still, no matter what happened, our festivals came around at the appointed time and we prepared to celebrate another New Year, which we hoped, optimistically, would be a sweeter one. It was hard to believe, but all our children were now grown-up. Shira Mazal was 22, a qualified teacher and dating a nice boy named Shimon from a Yemenite family. Naturally, this made Kobi and me very happy. It was too soon to know if they would be married, but already in my mind I was planning a henna ceremony.

Uri, now 20, had only one more year to complete his Army service and my baby, Moshe, was unbelievably 18 and about to enter the army.

It seemed such a short time ago that he was playing with toy airplanes. Although it felt disloyal, I often wondered how it would feel to live in a Western country where Army service was not mandatory, and 18-year-old kids could have fun, go to parties, be carefree, their biggest decision what they should pack for college and what career they should follow. Our boys couldn't think that far ahead, because the tragedy was that none of them knew if they would survive that long. But army service was a rite of passage in Israel. It was also a badge of honor and "conscientious objectors" were few and far between. Certainly we didn't know of any among Uri and Moshe's friends.

It was wonderful that the whole family would be together for Rosh Hashana as Uri had leave. We would also be hosting Yitzhak and Dina, Dikla and Menelik, their cute son Israel, and his little sister.

Our neighbors were going away for the holidays and had generously offered us the use of their apartment to house our guests from Rosh haAyin. I doubt if this would ever happen overseas, but in Israel it is common practice, especially in the settlements. Anyone going away on holidays offers his home to neighbors who are staying, so that they can invite their extended family. Of course, if they are later celebrating a bar-mitzvah, Shabbat Chatan (a bridegroom's Sabbath) or any other important occasion, it is expected and understood that the favor will be returned. It always is, even if the family deliberately has to leave home to make it vacant for a weekend if their friends have an important "simcha."

Our neighbors were a wonderful American family named Weiss, who had made aliyah three years earlier and loved their Old City apartment situated below ours. I was a bit nervous as Israel was a mischievous 5-year-old, and Dikla couldn't watch him every minute. I went in before they arrived and placed out of harm's way everything I could find that was breakable, like vases and ornaments, and anything he might regard as a toy, such as the TV remote control. I also made sure there was a big bowl of fruit, an urn of hot water, tea and coffee, and a home-made cake. The new baby was named Esther as she'd been born at Purim. She was not a problem as she just ate, cried and slept, much to her brother's disgust. He wasn't jealous of her, but just found her completely boring. "She doesn't DO anything," he informed me unhappily.

"All babies are like that. You were too."

He was indignant. "No, I wasn't. I'm a boy. I play. It's only girls who are so lazy." A true chauvinist in the making, but a very cute one. It seemed such a short time since his brit and next year he would be starting school.

Although Kobi and I had both been born in Israel, we still celebrated the New Year incorporating as many Yemenite traditions as we could. Our heritage was like a sacred tradition that we were proud of and felt obligated to pass on to our children. I think sometimes it embarrassed them, but they never said so if it did.

For a month, from the beginning of the Hebrew month of Elul, we had begun saying the penitential prayers, "Selichot." We called them "Ashmarot." They were eight psalms recited daily before dawn. Kobi had been rising at 5 a.m. every morning and taking a reluctant Moshe to synagogue with him. "I never knew there WAS a 5 a.m.," he would grumble when his father shook him to wake him up. At the Yemenite "minyan," the shofar that was blown was not the ram's horn, but a long, curly antelope's horn. We still owned this "dishon" that had been passed down to us from Ezra, our ancestor Mazal's husband, which he'd brought with him in the meager belongings when they left Yemen. It made a low, growling sound, more menacing than alarming.

On the eve of Rosh Hashana, Kobi always fasted as he remembered his father doing, but he never insisted on other family members doing likewise. He also visited the grave of Rav Shalom Sharabi, the Jerusalem kabbalist who was born in Sana'a, Yemen in 1720. He had become known as one of Jerusalem's greatest rabbis, and he was believed to be both a saint and a miracle worker. The legend has it that the Prophet Elijah actually appeared to him. He was buried on the Mount of Olives after he died at an early age of only 57. Kobi owned a copy of his prayerbook "Nehar Shalom," which details the secrets and mystical meditations on prayers, and commandments for the entire year.

We all prayed from a special Yemenite "machzor" that was a bit different from the Ashkenazi one. There were more psalms and we recited "Kol Klei Yozar" and read the Talmudic tractate Yoma. We had changed some of the customs because women wanted to hear the shofar blasts, which was forbidden in Yemen.

Shira Mazal had helped me prepare a wonderful meal, and Dina and Dikla had also brought treats with them. On my best snowy white tablecloth we'd set out the traditional symbols for a sweet New Year ... honey, pomegranates, figs and apples. I had baked bread in honor of the festival which was time-consuming, but the wonderful fragrance of freshly baked "challot" made it worth all the work. We were all dressed in white, and felt truly blessed as we ate the wonderful soup, roast chicken, baked vegetables and luscious fruits.

Menelik told us that back in Ethiopia, Rosh Hashana was known as "The Light is Rising". Instead of the shofar, or ram's horn, he remembers they clashed cymbals, which is understandable as Psalm 150 uses the word "truah" for a cymbal.

Different customs. Different rituals. But I had such a warm feeling as I surveyed our family ranged around the table. Kobi still limped, but he had survived two wars and his periods of depression seemed to have passed. Shira Mazal had grown into a beautiful young woman, who would probably marry before the next New Year came around. I had heard from some of her colleagues and even her students that she was a caring, excellent teacher, who loved her work. Uri looked handsome in his army uniform, but this night I was happy to see him in civilian clothes. He never complained how hard life was in the IDF, but sometimes he would come home on leave with such weariness etched in his young features that I would feel a physical ache as I kissed him. This would also be Moshe's last Rosh Hashana as a civilian, and I prayed that there would be peace so that he could come safely through his years of service.

As we sipped our wine, my eyes looked with affection on the new branch of our family ... Menelik, Dikla and their children. Their little boy had us all laughing at his antics, his grandparents obviously adored him and his baby sister sleeping peacefully in the next room. "I must count my blessings," I kept telling myself during the festive meal. "Tonight we are all together, all safe under one roof, in Jerusalem, the Holy City. May G-d continue to protect us against our enemies for another year, and may we all be inscribed in the Book of Life."

Chapter 21

THE YEAR ENDED WITH the death of Golda Meir. She had made mistakes as Prime Minister, just as every human being does. But we mourned her and the whole world paid tribute to this remarkable leader. Even President Sadat of Egypt acknowledged that she had been a great leader and an honest adversary. She had died of lymphoma, a disease that had been diagnosed 15 years earlier, but she had never complained or let it interfere with her duties. I think the women of Israel mourned her the most ... I know I did. She had risen to unbelievable heights in a man's world, and that was a remarkable accomplishment.

Three months later President Sadat signed a peace treaty with Prime Minister Menachem Begin, brokered by U.S. President Jimmy Carter at the White House. We prayed this would be a real "shalom," a genuine peace. The border between our two countries was opened, and Israeli tourists went to visit the pyramids, the Sphinx, and the Valley of the Kings.

Of course there is a price to pay for everything, and we had to give up Sinai and the Abu Rodeis oil fields. With a heavy heart I remembered a holiday many years earlier. It was the first holiday since our marriage that Kobi and I had been able to take without the children, and we spent a week at Di Zahav "the Golden," which the Arabs called Dahab.

It was the nearest thing to paradise that anyone could envisage. Even now, if I close my eyes, I can see it again ... a stretch of golden sand dotted with palm trees, bunches of dates hanging down, ripe for the picking. The Red Sea shimmering in bands of color ... azure, turquoise, deep midnight blue. A backdrop of stark, towering mountains. Cloudless skies.

We would go to the beach very early to watch the flaming, scarlet sunrise. Sometimes a camel would saunter over and gaze at us indifferently from under hooded eyes. After he sniffed us and decided we were inedible and uninteresting, he would wander off. He probably belonged to a Beduin, but we never saw his owner. We were told that they are a trusting people who customarily leave their animals and their property unguarded.

There was a Beduin boy who travelled on our bus for the three-hour, 146 kilometer trip south from Eilat, and Kobi thought the camel might belong to his family. He was a handsome lad, dark skin contrasting with his spotless white "keffiyeh" (Arab headdress). His intense black eyes reflected generations of scanning limitless desert horizons.

We stayed at the small moshav Di Zahav near the oasis of Dahab, one of the Biblical stopping-places of the Children of Israel during their journey across the desert towards the Promised Land. The moshav had only come into being seven years earlier, when the road came through from Eilat in 1972. Only 19 families lived there, plus a few singles. There was no hotel, just a collection of two-story bungalows and a small restaurant. There were also a few simple huts, a kiosk, and a diving center.

Now that we were losing this jewel, I tried to recapture the sensations I had felt during that idyllic week with my husband. I can feel the warmth of the sun on my body, the fragrance of the sea at dawn. The taste of salt on my lips after a swim. The mountains towering 6000 feet straight out of the sea. The ocean shimmering and the colors constantly changing and intensifying as we watched. Their secret depths vibrated with life ... coral reefs, sea anemones, giant clams, butterfly fish, groupers, sea turtles, and octopi.

There were few other tourists or Israelis there then, as most found it too isolated a spot. They preferred the commercial comforts of Eilat, a real tourist resort with luxury hotels and entertainment. There were just a handful of guests and we'd hear snatches of conversation in English, Hebrew, and Scandinavian languages that we didn't understand, but mostly we were happy to be on our own. I can even recall the music on the beach from someone's transistor radio. It was playing "Halleluyah," Israel's winning song entry in the recently-held Eurovision song contest. The lyrics were so appropriate: "Halleluyah" ... the universal word for giving praise to the Creator.

And now Di Zahav will soon be a memory. Maybe we won't even be able to visit it anymore, and certainly the moshav will be gone. But it will always stay in my memory, and also I'm sure in Kobi's, as "the Golden".

Chapter 22

PERHAPS IT WAS BECAUSE Kobi sensed a certain sadness in me, or maybe it was because of all the publicity that the peace treaty with Egypt had engendered, that he came up with a surprising suggestion.

"How would you like to visit Egypt?" he asked me one evening as we were closing "The Pomegranate Pendant."

I looked to see if he was joking. "I don't know. Isn't it kind of disloyal?"

"Israelis are going in droves. Aren't you curious?"

I hesitated. "I don't see too many Egyptian tourists coming to Israel. In fact I don't see any. So much for bilateral trade."

"True," he conceded. "But after all, as slaves we built their pyramids. I'd like to see our ancestors' handiwork."

To me it was a strange idea. We thanked the Almighty for delivering us from Egyptian bondage every Passover. Would it be right to go back there voluntarily? However I could see that Kobi was excited about the idea and remembering his bouts of depression after fighting in Israel's wars, it seemed cruel to put a damper on his enthusiasm. I agreed we could go for a week.

Although I wasn't really very keen, his excitement began to infect me. Each evening he would read up on what life was like for Jews there before the Exodus, and soon I entered into the spirit of his research.

This is what we learned: Ancient Egypt had three periods of history: the Old Kingdom, which comprised the first ten dynasties of pyramid builders ending in 2500 BCE; the Middle Kingdom from 11th to 17th dynasty extending from 2500 to 1587 BCE, an obscure period when the Hyksos, Beduin invaders from the Arabian Desert, ruled Egypt. They were expelled by the founder of the 18th dynasty in 1587 BCE. This ushered in the New Kingdom until the end of the 20th dynasty in 1100 BCE. Later Egypt came under Libyan, Persian, Macedonian, and Roman rule.

Biblical interest in Egypt begins during the time of the Middle Kingdom. Joseph served a Pharaoh who was one of the Hyksos kings, a ruler who restored and enlarged the temples and encouraged learning. Later, native rulers who followed him tried to eradicate every trace of the Hyksos, so this period is obscure and it is hard to be certain of Egyptian chronology.

Not long after Joseph's death, the Hyksos were driven back into Asia and a native ruler regained the throne. This nationalist dynasty was a calamity for the Israelites, the descendants of Jacob. As friends of the overthrown Hyksos kings, they lost their favored position and all their past services were ignored. From prosperous settlers in the eastern delta of the Nile, the Jews gradually were forced into slavery, with each ruler issuing harsher decrees. The rulers were great architects, measuring their fame by the number and magnificence of their monuments.

This great frenzy of building naturally called for forced labor. The feared and hated Hebrews were the natural choice. They were condemned to cruel slavery as bricklayers and navvies. It was particularly cruel because their nature and tradition was to be shepherds. We are unsure who was the "new king" who initiated their oppression, as "Pharaoh" was the royal title for every king. The Jews dwelt in Goshen, but the Egyptian chroniclers mostly ignored the slaves. Even as shepherds they were despised. Kobi read me from Genesis 46:34: "Thy servants have been keepers of cattle from our youth even until now, both we and our fathers, that ye may dwell in the land of Goshen; for every shepherd is an abomination to the Egyptians."

The Egyptian name for the Hebrews was "Apuriu," and there are few references to them on the monuments. But in a report addressed to an official in the reign of Rameses III, it is written: "Give corn to the native soldiers, and also to the Apuriu who are bringing up stones for the great tower of Pa-Ramessu."

The Egyptian records pass over the entire Exodus in silence, which is always their custom in defeat. Even the Hyksos conquest of Egypt, the most important political event in their history, is not mentioned on their monuments.

The scholars Kobi researched identified the Pharaoh of our oppression as Rameses II, extravagant and a tyrant. He reigned 1300 – 1234 BCE. Evidently he was vain and boastful, and covered the land with constructions on which his name was engraved thousands of times, detailing great conquests which he never made. The Exodus took place under his son Merneptah.

Many thousands of years have passed since the Exodus, but still I felt strange to be contemplating a trip to Egypt, just as I would have felt to revisit scenes from the Holocaust. Still, I kept my reservations to myself, as Kobi deserved a holiday. He was not one for the usual tourist resorts.

We could have flown to Egypt, but decided to go overland by bus to see as much as possible. We left Jerusalem at 8 a.m. on a surprisingly sunny day. Our coach sped through the Judean Hills, past Latrun and on towards Ashkelon. Three hours later, we were crossing the Sinai Desert, past exotic black tents and shanties of the Beduin. Mile after mile of sand dunes, the only signs of life were the herds of goats and an occasional camel.

At Neot Sinai, we crossed the border into Egypt, a procedure that took a frustrating four hours. Kobi joked: "Now you know why the Children of Israel wandered the desert for 40 years. They spent 39 of them waiting to cross the border!" Eventually the formalities were over, and we boarded an Egyptian bus, crossing large desert tracts like those we had passed in Israel, until we reached the Suez Canal.

Because of all the travelling and delays at the border, it was now dark. We had to wait for the ferry with a large crowd that had gathered ... Beduin from Sinai, tourists from Israel and other countries, as well as local Egyptians. We passed the time chatting with some of them and watching a convoy of ships sail by, en route to Europe, Greece and Turkey.

It was midnight when we reached Cairo, a city of 10 million people – more than double the whole population of Israel. We couldn't believe the traffic ... people not only crowded on buses, but actually hanging out the windows or sitting on the roof. Our hotel was called "Scheherezade"... a very opulent lobby of marble and crystal chandeliers. Our room was clean and quite attractive, but almost nothing worked ... the bathroom had no soap nor plug for the bath; when Kobi turned on the light switch, he was nearly electrocuted as a shock sent him reeling; the bed lamps had no globes in them.

Still, we hadn't expected five star luxury, and we made a joke of it. At least we had a view, as our room overlooked the Nile, winding through the city like a silver ribbon. Most of our interest in Egypt was linked to its Jewish history, so we spent the first day visiting two synagogues. The first was the Ben Ezra synagogue. A Jewess, a very old lady named Mme. Argami showed us around. She said she did it regularly since the opening of the border had brought an influx of Jewish visitors. The site of the synagogue had seen much conflict and change. The original was torn down and replaced with a Roman fortress and then a church. The present synagogue dates from the 12th century and is old and musty, weary with disuse.

She took us down a flight of stairs to some murky water where, legend has it, Moses was plucked from the bulrushes by Pharaoh's daughter. We wanted to believe it, but it hardly seemed a place a fastidious princess would choose to bathe.

Prior to 1948, she told us the congregation numbered 2,000. Today, she said there were just 140, all very old. "Why don't you come to Israel?" I couldn't help asking.

"I have visited," she told us, "but I want to live out my life here. We're not discriminated against," she insisted.

When we wondered how the synagogue was maintained, Mme. Argami informed us it was by gifts from America, the Joint Distribution Committee, organizations and philanthropists in Israel and Europe. "For Passover, they send matzot and Haggadot from Israel, and wonderful Manischewitz wine from America."

In the afternoon, we visited "Sha'ar haShamayim" (Gate of Heaven) synagogue on Adly Street. Large and ornate, it looked more like a museum. It was hard to imagine anyone actually praying there despite the fact it boasts 18 Sifrei Torah (Scrolls of the Law). It was under repair, but we were told that it should be ready by Purim, when President Sadat had been invited. They didn't know if he would accept.

More interesting than Cairo was Alexandria, "The

Pearl of Egypt", where Cleopatra had ruled, become Caesar's lover and borne him a son, and where she lived with Marc Anthony until she killed herself in 31 BCE, ending Greek rule. It is Egypt's largest port and an international holiday resort, although the villas lining the beach-front are shabby, with paint peeling from the shutters. There was also a synagogue there, but it only had 40 members, the youngest of whom was 65. We were told that all the women had married Arabs and converted to Islam.

Of course the most interesting part of the trip was visiting Memphis and Giza, the Sphinx and the pyramids ... massive structures built by our forefathers when they were slaves. We walked to the top of one of the pyramids. There was a narrow dark staircase, and it was very claustrophobic. Outside, the locals were trying to sell all kinds of kitsch to the tourists, but although we bought a few souvenirs to give our kids, there was nothing suitable for our store. The merchants had developed a wonderful patter to engender laughter and generosity in the visitors. One evil-looking guy with broken teeth grabbed Kobi's sleeve. "I will give you two camels for your wife," he offered. Kobi replied: "I'll have to think it over. I don't really have a place to keep them at home." Fortunately, I have a sense of humor or I'd have hit him.

As darkness fell, I felt an enormous surge of excitement. We re-crossed the border and returned to the place that held everything I loved in my life, Eretz Israel.

Chapter 23

I REMEMBER THE OPENING of Tolstoy's "Anna Karenina...All families are unhappy in their own way." Perhaps we had just been lucky, but I'd always felt we had a happy family. Of course, there were the usual squabbles when the kids were small, Moshe would kick his brother; Uri would tease him until he cried; Shira Mazal would spend too much time in the bathroom while her brothers pounded on the door ... but these were small things. Kobi's periods of depression had cast a cloud on the family when he'd come back from fighting or reserve duty, but in time we overcame these difficult periods.

So, when unhappiness deluged our family like a flood, I did not know how to handle it. It caught me completely off-guard and for a few minutes I was at a loss for words. The bombshell came one evening just as we were finishing dinner.

"Well Uri, two weeks from now you'll be finished your army service. Have you decided what you want to study and whether you want to go to Hebrew University or Bar-Ilan?" I was really just making conversation. He had plenty of time before the new academic year began.

He paused before answering. "Actually, neither."

I felt a tremor of fear, but wouldn't acknowledge it. "You mean you want a holiday first? That's OK. Nearly everyone does that, although I hope you won't go to the Far East like thousands of Israelis do. You could go to Eilat, or the Galilee, or even Europe if you want to..." I kept on talking to quieten the sense of foreboding that was growing in the room.

"I mean I'm going to study overseas. New York. I've applied and been accepted to City College for a B.A. in Business Administration, and then I'll do an M.B.A."

"But that will take years," I gasped. "You arranged all this without even telling us?"

I turned to Kobi, but he wouldn't meet my eyes. The room was deathly quiet.

"You knew?" I addressed them all accusingly.

Uri said quietly, " I was waiting for the right time to tell you."

"Why are you doing this? Why are you leaving Israel, your birthplace, the Jewish homeland?" I was aware that my voice was screeching, tears running down my cheeks, but I no longer cared. "You can't. I forbid it. Say something!" I demanded of his father.

Kobi tried to put a consoling hand on my arm, but I pushed it away savagely. "He's nearly 21, Bracha. He's an adult."

"Am I going mad? I don't understand. Why New York? What's in New York?"

"A normal life," he answered quietly.

"What, dollars?" I demanded. "Movies, luxuries, discos, the fast lane? Are those the values we've taught you?"

No one would meet my eyes. Shira Mazal was also crying now. Moshe was attacking his food. Kobi was staring at the floor.

"I can't take it any more. I've done my share. I've had three years of army service, and seen more violence than kids my age overseas see in their whole lives. I've seen boys die ... Arab boys and Jewish boys ... whose lives haven't even started yet. My friend Roi only has one leg. Three of my friends have died. They never had a chance to study, to marry, to have a family. If I stay, I'll have to do reserve duty for at least another 20 years. I want a chance to have some fun. I think I've earned it. And now Moshe's going in the army. I don't want to be here to wonder every minute where he is, if he's safe, if he's coming home, if he's still in one piece…" It was more than I'd ever heard Uri say before.

"You won't think about your brother while you're in America?" I asked sarcastically.

"Imma, you're not trying to understand. There'll be distractions. I can prepare for a career. I can make plans, have dates, fulfill dreams. I can go on vacation. I won't have to listen to the news every hour to find out if fighting has broken out and I need to rejoin my unit." Uri was trying not to cry, but I couldn't feel anything for him at that moment. Only contempt. Contempt, for my own son, of whom I'd been proud and loved every day of his life until now.

"Do you understand any of this?" I asked my husband angrily.

"Yes I do," he replied quietly. "Do you think I didn't have the same thoughts at times? Do you think there was one man fighting with me who didn't have the same thoughts. Survival is the most basic, natural instinct in the world. Many times I wanted to take you and the children to a safer place … a place where they would never have to experience blood and violence as part of their lives…"

"But you didn't. You kept going because you're an Israeli. Your country is worth fighting for, worth sacrificing for. You never deserted it."

Shira Mazal pushed back her chair and left the table. Moshe mumbled something and followed her. There were just the three of us.

"I am so disappointed," I finally said, exhausted from all the emotion. "When are you leaving?"

"In three weeks."

I nodded. There was nothing else to say. I needed to be alone, so I left the house, stepping out into the velvet darkness of the Old City, and firmly closed the door behind me.

Chapter 24

BY NOW IT WAS close to midnight, but I felt a tremendous need to go to the Kotel, the Western Wall. Even at this hour, it was not deserted. Both on the men's and women's side, there were a few stray souls, possibly in as much anguish as I was.

"Lord of the Universe," I prayed, my hands caressing the cold stone, "help me bear this tragedy. Watch over my headstrong son, wherever his feet may take him. Help our family to feel whole again."

Usually, a feeling of peace would descend on me after I prayed at the Kotel, but this night I still felt restless and wounded. My mind kept going back over years of conversations with Uri, trying to see if there was something I might have said or inferred to cause him to reach such a decision. The word "yored" is an embarrassment. Someone who has left Israel for greener pastures. There were many reasons for leaving, and I had never blamed or judged anyone before. But I couldn't be objective now. He was my elder son. What if he influenced Moshe also?

I walked home via our store, "The Pomegranate Pendant." The windows were lit, displaying all the rich treasures of our stock. "Mazal and Ezra came to Eretz Israel from Yemen to found a family," I thought sadly. "Through disease and death, poverty and war, they remained steadfast. Now it is my son who will break the chain. He wants a 'normal' life. But life has never been 'normal' for the Jews. There have always been pogroms and persecution, anti-Semitism, rejection, crusades and inquisitions, no matter where they settled. Finally, we have our own country, our own State, where he is a free citizen, and voluntarily he wants to leave!"

I must have been a strange sight, standing in the street of Jerusalem's Old City in the early morning hours, looking in the window of our store. It was probably dangerous to be a woman alone at that hour in that place, but I was too weary to care. I was glad no one had followed me ... not my husband nor children ... because I didn't want to listen to platitudes, or have any conversation at all.

They were all asleep, or pretending to be, when I got home. I couldn't find any rest, even though I was physically and emotionally exhausted. I tossed and turned all night.

The next morning, we all seemed to be avoiding each other, or maybe they were just avoiding me. I know I looked tight-lipped and angry. Usually Kobi and I went to work together, but after a few minutes' hesitation, when he saw I was not getting ready, he left the house on his own. I decided to work in my garden for a while, to calm myself. There is no activity more peaceful and therapeutic than working in the garden, weeding, planting, watering, pruning.

The garden has become my private refuge where I satisfy my need for beauty, tranquillity and achievement. It is my link with nature. In each plant lies the balance and harmony of the living world. In the growth of a seed, to a seedling, and then to full blossom, the miracle of life itself is revealed.

As I worked, I felt my anger slowly ebbing away. In its place I felt instead a profound sadness. It wasn't just that my son was leaving home, for I remember a poster I had on my own wall as a teenager. It showed a bird, soaring through the sky. Underneath was written: "If you love someone, let him go free. If he returns, he is yours. If he doesn't, he never was."

What Uri planned to do was much more than leave home. He was leaving his homeland. It is hard to explain the emotion involved to anyone who is not Israeli, for this ancient land is also a new land that came into being only in 1948. But its birth was the fulfillment and realization of a dream for the whole Jewish people. Never again would they be forced to wander the earth, begging hostile nations to take them in. It was a haven for Jews who were being persecuted; but also a promised land for those who came freely, wanting to live among their own people, wanting to contribute something. It is a harsh land, but you can survive here. More than that, you can thrive and feel proud.

I laid down my trowel and was sitting on the tiny patch of grass when my downstairs American neighbor Bella Weiss came out with her shopping basket.

"Not at work?" she asked, surprised to see me home at that hour.

"No, I don't think I'll go to the store today."

"Is something wrong?" she asked gently.

Unable to speak, I suddenly found myself crying. She sat down beside me, putting her arms around me. An older woman, it felt like my mother holding me. "Uri's going to live in America" I finally managed to tell her.

"Well, that's not so bad, is it? America's a wonderful place. I was born there."

"That's the point. He was born in Israel. This is where he belongs."

"Oh my dear, very few people these days end up where they started from. Israel itself is a melting-pot of people from every corner of the globe. He probably just wants to see the world. Israel is just a tiny dot on the map, after all. Let him get the travel bug out of his system and maybe he'll come back again."

I shook my head. "It's not the travel bug, I could understand that. He doesn't want to fight in any more wars."

"Of course he doesn't. Who does? He did his share, for three long years," she reminded me. "He's not a coward."

"But what will happen to him in New York? What will he become?"

"Probably a very successful man. You know my daughter and grandchildren are still there. They hope to make aliyah eventually, when the time is right for them. They are very Zionistic. I've got a grandson, Danny, his age, and a granddaughter Zelda, just a bit younger. I'll ask them to look out for him." I nodded gratefully. "There's a vibrant Jewish community there," Bella reminded me, "he won't come to any harm. Give him your blessings. Don't part in anger and bitterness."

Of course she was right. We don't own our children. I would try to swallow my pain, and let him know I would always be his mother and love him, wherever he was.

Chapter 25

I TRIED TO IMPROVE my behavior for the short time that was left, even helping him with his packing and being as affectionate as I could manage. It seemed the whole family was walking on eggshells ... Uri trying to be considerate by not discussing his future plans; Kobi and the children treating me with the kind of compassion one extends to an invalid, which annoyed me more than consoled me.

I did leave the newspaper placed prominently on Uri's desk which had a front-page article about the Mount Scopus campus of the Hebrew University re-opening after 31 years, but if he read it, he made no comment.

I realized I was waging a losing battle, but could not accept his departure.

I was pleased when Bella said that her daughter and her family would invite him for Shabbat meals as they lived within reasonable walking distance of the Manhattan apartment he had rented in New York.

In vain I analyzed every word of Uri's letters home those first few months, trying to detect any trace of homesickness. At first, he wrote only about settling in; his two Israeli roommates; and the courses he was taking at City College ... he enjoyed the lectures. He was teaching Hebrew on Sunday mornings at a Talmud Torah to earn pocket money; he had visited the Weiss family's daughter, Leah and her husband Ethan Weinberg, with their children Danny and Zelda. He asked a few questions about what Moshe was doing in the army, but I got the feeling it was more out of politeness than any deep concern for the family.

As the months went by, his enthusiasm for New York became even stronger, and his disconnectedness from Jerusalem more evident. His letters were peppered with place names like Battery Park, West Street, the World Trade Center, Versey and Liberty Streets. He could see the Hudson River and the Statue of Liberty from his bedroom window, and sometimes he took the Hoboken Ferry. He loved visiting the World Financial Center with its famous name stores, gift shops, and business services. The names meant nothing to me, but when I shared some of his letters with Bella, she was impressed that he had bought his sister a blouse from Ann Taylor; his father a shirt from Barney's New York, and that he frequented Rizzoli Bookstore. New York, according to Uri, was dazzling and exciting, with symphony concerts in the Winter Garden with its sixteen palm trees; museums; Broadway shows … It throbbed, pulsated with life and action. He was certainly not homesick!

In contrast, my letters to him sounded dull and boring. We were all OK; Dikla's children were growing older and were very cute; the store was doing well. Israel's "Milk and Honey" pop group had won the Eurovision Song Contest. I don't know what his father, Shira Mazal or Moshe wrote to him about, or how often. I don't think they envied him, and they certainly never said so, but perhaps secretly they did. Jerusalem, after all, was not New York.

But Jerusalem was something else. It was not just a maze of streets and buildings like other cities. It was an emotion. Yehuda Amichai, the great Israeli poet, wrote that the air was thick with prayers and dreams, and like the air over industrial cities, it was hard to breathe. We did live our daily lives like citizens the world over, yet there was always the consciousness of something more, especially in the Old City. So much of it had been restored, and it was amazing to visit shops in the Cardo, and to be aware of the history under our feet. We walked on stones where kings and prophets had trodden. We could raise our eyes to Har haBayit, the Temple Mount, and imagine what it was like when the Temple stood there, when pilgrims would make their three-times-a-year journey to bring sacrifices. Jerusalem was unique. There were other cities more exciting, more breathtakingly beautiful, but no other city more holy, more sanctified, more beloved.

Yet still, Uri did not return, except for two weeks when his sister got married. It was a bittersweet time. We loved Shimon, from a Yemenite background as we were, and he was the bridegroom every family hopes for when their daughter marries. Our families were friends; he was a good-looking boy now studying for a law degree and also working part-time; they had known each other for many years, even from B'nei Akiva as teenagers. He had completed his army service, but it hadn't left him scarred the way it had Uri and even my husband. Uri had been voluble about it; Kobi had his occasional periods of depression. I read an article by a psychologist that it was probably due to post-traumatic stress syndrome, but whenever I had suggested therapy, he had rejected it quite strongly. "Of course I'll remember what I've seen and experienced for the rest of my life, and probably re-live it. I don't really want to forget it or the friends I lost. They deserve to be remembered!"

Perhaps Shimon's army service had been much less traumatic as he'd served in Intelligence, or maybe it was his sunny nature, but he seemed less complicated and moody than the other men in our family, which boded well for our daughter's happiness. A wedding is an emotionally bonding time between a mother and daughter. It was fun to go with her to choose the fabric and style for her wedding gown; her hairdo; the flowers; buy pretty lingerie for her trousseau; even to pass on favorite recipes. These are boring details for men who can't really understand what all the fuss is about, and for whom it only becomes a reality once the invitations have been posted, and the financial side needed to be calculated.

Still, Shira Mazal's happiness did have an effect on all of us. She had her henna ceremony two days before the wedding, just as her namesake would have wanted, and I fastened around her neck the pomegranate pendant that our forefather Ezra had fashioned for his bride a hundred years ago in Yemen. It signified so much more for the ben-Yichya family and all its branches. It was still a symbol of fertility that carried that blessing with it for the wearer, but it had an even deeper significance in our family. It was a symbol of the love that had existed between our great grandparents; the hope of a newer and better life in Eretz Israel than they had known in Yemen with its persecution and poverty. It was the name they had given to their store, that supported first their children, and generations later, still gave us financial security. We were like links in the golden chain on which the pomegranate had been suspended. Everyone knows that a chain is only as strong as its weakest link, and I felt that Uri had weakened our chain of loyalty and tradition.

Still, he was our son, and even for a brief visit, it was wonderful to have him home. I made a vow to myself that I would not spoil it by tears or pleading, or even a hint of recrimination. He looked wonderful … strong, athletic, relaxed, well-dressed. I believe "cool" was the trendy description. He had brought us all gifts and I'm sure they represented a sacrifice because although we were paying for his studies, he earned his own pocket money which couldn't have been much. He taught Hebrew and in the summer worked as a waiter in one of the Jewish resorts in the Catskills. I suspect that Kobi occasionally sent him some extra money, but he never told me and I didn't really want to know. Why make it easier for him to live so far away, not just in distance but also in tradition.

Shimon invited him to be his best man at the wedding, and for that short period, our family felt whole again. I didn't wake up every morning with that hollow sensation that had plagued me since he left. Only another mother could understand the feeling.

We had one conversation alone the night before he left, and it was Uri who initiated it.

"It's been a wonderful visit. Thank you for not laying the guilt on me."

"Well, as your father said, you're an adult. We don't own you. You have to make your own decisions."

He nodded. "It was right for me. My army service had traumatized me. At the time, I had to get away, to a completely different environment."

"And now?"

He hesitated. "I don't say that it's forever. People change. Circumstances change. But for now, it's very good for me. I have lots of new friends. My studies are going well. I've begun my Master's and I feel very fulfilled."

"Are all your friends American?" I asked sadly.

"What you're really asking is, 'Are they all Jewish?'."
I nodded. "No, they're not all Jewish, but you don't need to worry. I only date Jewish girls. I still keep Shabbat and 'kashrut'. Maybe I'm not as religious as I used to be, but 'Yiddishkeit' is still important to me." He leaned over and squeezed my hand. "I won't do anything to make you ashamed, Imma. You and Abba gave me too strong a ba-

sis for that."

It was the most comforting talk we'd had in a very long time. He had answered all the questions I'd been afraid to ask. Even if he did not come back to live in Israel, he would not disgrace us. He would graduate and make us proud. The hollow feeling in my chest began slowly to close up.

Chapter 26

1985 WAS A YEAR of miracles, at least for our family. Life is like that. I've always believed that it goes in cycles. We have bad patches, and then we move into the sunshine. Maybe it is only because of the periodic darkness that we can truly appreciate it when radiant light finally breaks through. I remember a quotation from Rabbi Aharon of Apt: "Light is known to exist by virtue of darkness. One is the chair upon which the other sits."

The year began with Operation Moses, from November 1984 to January 1985. In that time, 15,000 Ethiopian Jews were brought to Israel, finally coming home to the land they had been praying for and dreaming of throughout centuries of privation, pain and persecution. Learning about them was a new experience for most Israelis, but because of Menelik, we knew a great deal. Although a number of Falashas had been forced to convert, even they had remained true to Judaism in their hearts. Like our Yemenite forefathers, the Beta Israel were a gentle people, at first overwhelmed by the strangeness of this ancient and new land, where we wore Western clothes, used washing machines, and watched television.

There were many tragedies amongst the stories we heard. "Operation Moses" was the collective name for the secret Mossad operations, carried out in collaboration with the Israeli Navy in the heart of enemy country, Sudan. Just over a short period, 15,000 Jews were spirited out of Ethiopia on IAF planes or rubber Navy boats in amazing secrecy. Finally Menelik's family came, except for one brother Jacob, who died tragically en route. But we welcomed his parents, Rachel and Isaac Bogale and his two sisters, Meskie and Inbal. They had walked – two hungry, danger-filled weeks – from a humble village to the Sudanese border. For two nights, they hid in a hut. Inbal needed to be hospitalized at first, for weakness, malnutrition and a parasite not seen before in Israel, but she recovered quickly.

We all went with Menelik and Dikla to the airport to welcome them. They arrived wearing their traditional garments, with no possessions or money. There were many Ethiopians among the crowd looking for parents and siblings, with tears in their eyes when they were not to be found. But there were also cries of delight and excitement when some were reunited with relatives they believed had died in Ethiopia or Sudan.

We were almost crying ourselves as we watched Menelik embrace his family. Of course we couldn't understand what was being said, but we saw his parents' look of disbelief as he showed them first his wife, Dikla, and then his children. They were obviously shaken that she was not black as they were, but when she shyly took their hands and kissed them, they broke into radiant smiles and bent down and hugged the two children. As he reassured them that they were indeed welcome in our family, and that they would even be able to work in their traditional crafts for our store, it was like a light illuminated their faces. What was truly heartwarming was to see Yitzhak and Dina, Dikla's parents, open their arms to the newcomers in a gesture of welcome and acceptance.

It was only a few months later that more miracles

occurred. First, we became grandparents. Shira Mazal and Shimon had their first child, a daughter. They named her Ruchama, after my great-aunt, Mazal's daughter. I was touched and grateful, for Ruchama had been a very special lady – an artist, and a sensitive and loving woman who taught me about herbs and flowers, and why it was important to take the time to look for the dewdrop in the heart of the rose.

The baby was so beautiful, a true Yemenite with olive skin, big dark eyes and a mop of black, curly hair. To hold your first grandchild in your arms is a joy that is beyond description. It is your child's child, your future, and a great blessing to have been spared long enough to witness such a happy occasion. When we left the hospital after seeing her for the first time, both Kobi and I were too overcome with emotion even to speak.

Our son Moshe was also the source of great pride. Now aged 25, he had decided to make the army his career and was an officer in "Kever." He looked distinguished and handsome in his uniform. We didn't know a great deal about his duties, because he couldn't discuss them, which we understood, but he was contributing to the defence of Israel and he deeply believed in what he was doing. He had many friends and when he was home, the house was filled with enthusiastic young voices and laughter. So much to be thankful for!

Even from Uri we heard good news. At first it came in hints in his letters. Zelda's name, Bella's American granddaughter, cropped up frequently whenever he referred to some place he had visited or a show he had seen. I asked Bella about it. "Oh, they are dating quite seriously," she told me. "She writes to us about Uri too. I can tell she likes him very much."

So it looked like he would marry an American. Well, it would not have been my choice, but at least she was

from a good family, and with her grandparents in Jerusalem, perhaps they would visit often.

Then came the letter that had me laughing and crying in turn:

My dear Imma and Abba,

"I have some news I want to share with you
that I think will make you very happy. Zelda has
agreed to marry me. However, she made one con-
dition. Her family is making aliyah in two months,
and she wants to come too. It is her dream to live
in Israel and it's my dream to marry Zelda. So I
have found a wonderful job with an American com-
pany that wants to open a branch in Israel. Once I
sign the contract, I'll give you all the details. For
now I can just say it is a managerial position that
will involve short, periodic trips back to America,
but it will be based in ... Jerusalem! So we plan to
be married in Jerusalem, and I'll have the best of
both worlds. I think this will make you happy?"

Happy! I was ecstatic. I rang all the family, almost
incoherent with excitement. I now knew what it meant
when people talked about their hearts singing.

Two months flew by, and it was Spring, almost Passover. The Winter bulbs I had planted miraculously
bloomed ... tulips, daffodils, and creamy pink freesias that
sent their heady perfume into the night air. My little herb
garden provided us with wonderful savory additions to our
food and all kinds of natural remedies I had learned from
Ruchama, who had learned them from her mother Mazal,
in this same patch of garden in Jerusalem's Old City.

Then Zelda and her parents arrived on aliyah, and a
day later, we were at the airport again to meet Uri. This

time it was not a visit. He had come home. "Blessed art Thou, O Lord our G-d, King of the Universe, Who has kept us alive, sustained us, and enabled us to reach this season."

Zelda endeared herself to us from the first. She was not Yemenite, but she was a pretty girl with a delightful smile and a warmth that immediately dissipated the nervousness I was feeling. Her hair was a shining chestnut color, accentuated by the lemon and beige suit she was wearing. She held out her hand to show me her engagement ring, a small emerald surrounded by tiny diamond chips.

"If you would like me to, I'd be happy to have a henna ceremony," she offered. And so it was. We hired a hall with a garden and all the family came. How many strands there were, emanating from my great grandparents. Mazal and Ezra ben-Yechiya who had been married a century ago in Sana'a, Yemen. They had brought their dreams to Eretz Israel, and although Ezra had died young, at least he had lived to see three children born, and established his store "The Pomegranate Pendant" as a showcase for the exquisite jewelry he fashioned.

Against the throbbing Yemenite music, I looked at my family. It was like a mosaic. There were dark Yemenites as we were; fair-skinned Ashkenazim; swarthy Sephardim; black Ethiopians. And now a lovely American girl standing next to my beloved son Uri, at a table strewn with flowers. I went up to her, carrying the mazbera bowl of the ground-up seeds and leaves of the henna plant.

I recited a prayer in her honor. Then I made a circle of henna on her palm, explaining it was a seal on her hand and her heart. She would always be a blessed member of our family. I dabbed henna on Uri's palm too, and those of Zelda's family. Finally, I unfastened the pomegranate pendant from around my neck and placed it around hers.

As I did so, my mind flashed back to my own "Chinah" when I tried to return the golden necklace to my great grandmother, Mazal.

"I want you to keep it," she had told me, "I am giving you a sacred trust. Every bride in the ben-Yechiya family should wear it at her henna ceremony, even if they don't marry Yemenites. Out of respect for my memory, try to keep the tradition. Tradition is very precious. No one should ever forget where they came from."

And now I was passing it on to Zelda, Uri's bride. "The pomegranate with its many seeds symbolizes fruitfulness," I explained, as Mazal had explained to me. "I hope you will be blessed with many children and that there will be many weddings in the family. May Mazal's pomegranate pendant continue to be a talisman for good, for all the generations yet to come."

Zelda kissed my cheek. "I am proud to wear it," she told me, and in that instant I felt such fulfillment washing over me that I had no words to express it.

The pomegranate pendant had indeed been a talisman for good, and we were all links in its golden chain. From far and wide we had returned to our homeland, the cradle of our faith. No matter what tribulations might be waiting in our future, tonight we were together in Jerusalem, under the stars shimmering like diamonds in the night sky. We could see the turrets and domes of the Old City walls surrounding us like an embrace. Orange blossom and jasmine perfumed the air. I watched my family dancing and celebrating together. Under my breath, I was reciting the 23rd Psalm:"

"… My cup runneth over.
Surely goodness and mercy shall follow me
All the days of my life.
And I shall dwell in the house of the Lord forever."

Jerusalem At Night

Black velvet spangled with stars
Is night in Jerusalem.

Splashes of gold -
The sigh of the wind -

An ancient perfume,
A taste of nectar.

Skyline of turrets and domes
Is night in Jerusalem.

Pine trees are whispering;
Thru' a tracery of leaves

Silver lights dot
A midnight canvas.

Landscape of enchantment
Is night in Jerusalem.

Bibliography

Those were the years, Nissim Mishal
The Beautiful People of the Book, Colette Berman &
    Yosef Miller
Operation Moses, Tuelor Parfitt
Front Page Israel, The Jerusalem Post
Israel at 50, Israel Ministry of Foreign Affairs